As both an educator and a follower of Christ, I appreciate resources that faithfully connect biblical truth with practical guidance for raising and teaching children. I gladly recommend this book to parents and teachers who strive to follow God's command to "train up a child in the way he should go" (Proverbs 22:6). Scripture and the principles of Love and Logic are beautifully woven together with real-life examples that make each principle clear, practical, and encouraging for those seeking to guide children with wisdom and grace. It is a book I will share with the families and teachers at my school.

Sandra Jolly, PhD, early childhood principal, Westminster Catawba Christian School

Dr. Fay's resources have uplifted our family for many years. We are confident that the wisdom and practicality in this book will encourage and bless your family as it has ours.

Charles and Samantha George, parents and business leaders

Raising Spiritually Strong Kids has been a huge encouragement to us as we raise our boys. We love how Dr. Fay combines psychological insight with biblical truth, sharing relatable stories from his own experience as a father. His teaching reminds parents to lead by example—even when we make mistakes—and to keep returning to God's way, especially in the hard moments. Grounded in Scripture and years of research, this book is very practical and helpful in everyday parenting. We finished the book feeling better equipped as parents and would recommend it to any parent who wants to grow in raising their kids in a godly way.

Scott and Cassie Bostick, parents and Christian missionaries

This book captures something many parents feel but don't always know how to articulate: Our role is not to control our children or their faith, but to faithfully reflect God's love and strength as they discover Him for themselves. Dr. Fay offers practical wisdom rooted in truth, equipping parents to lead with both grace and conviction. This is a powerful resource for anyone who desires to raise children who don't just behave well but genuinely know God. And if you're like me, your inner child just might receive healing and affirmation in the process.

Christine D'Clario, award-winning recording artist and worship leader, and mental health coach and advocate

This is the book we have been waiting for! Essential reading for parents and anyone who works with families, this book beautifully combines a solid, Christ-centered foundation with the well-established Love and Logic parenting approach. Dr. Fay's practical steps and personal stories make the concepts both accessible and immediately useful. I highly recommend this book to any parent seeking to strengthen their family's faith while cultivating healthy, connected relationships with their children.

Kimberly Dean, LMFT, pastor of LifeCare Ministries—Kids and Teens, Crossings Community Church

It was a joy to review Dr. Fay's book *Raising Spiritually Strong Kids*. In an age when we see kids walking away from faith in Jesus, this practical guide provides both the spiritual basis and the practical advice, with examples, to help parents raise kids who experience God's faithfulness in their lives.

Clint Zimmerman, MD, pediatrician, cofounder and owner of Blue Ridge Pediatric and Adolescent Medicine

This book is a refreshing and Spirit-filled reminder of God's faithfulness. With deep biblical truth and practical wisdom, Dr. Charles Fay encourages readers to trust Him more fully in every season of life. Through rich biblical insight and heartfelt storytelling, Dr. Fay draws readers closer to Christ and reminds us of God's unwavering grace. Our school has been using the principles of Love and Logic for twenty-five years, and now I highly recommend this book. It is a must-read for everyone, especially those who are longing to grow in their relationship with God while helping their children discover their own personal relationship with Christ.

Ralph H. Frier, executive director, Ridgeview Global Studies Academy

As a parent serving cross-culturally, I know how challenging it can be to raise spiritually strong kids without the support of familiar systems and community. *Raising Spiritually Strong Kids* offers a refreshing, practical approach rooted in empathy, respect, and natural consequences. Drawing from the trusted Love and Logic philosophy, Dr. Charles Fay writes with warmth and wisdom, equipping parents to guide their children toward responsibility and spiritual resilience—no matter where in the world God has called them. This book is an encouraging and deeply helpful resource for mission-minded families.

Mark Bruner, vice president of mobilization/field ministries, Avant Ministries

Dr. Charles Fay's *Raising Spiritually Strong Kids* is a timely and encouraging reminder that parents are the primary influencers of their children's faith. With clarity and practical wisdom, Dr. Fay emphasizes the importance of building a strong spiritual foundation in ways that feel both accessible and unintimidating. This book equips families with meaningful, everyday strategies to nurture lasting faith.

Kimberly Bastin, lower school assistant principal at Crossings Christian School

TYNDALE
REFRESH™

Think Well. Live Well. Be Well.

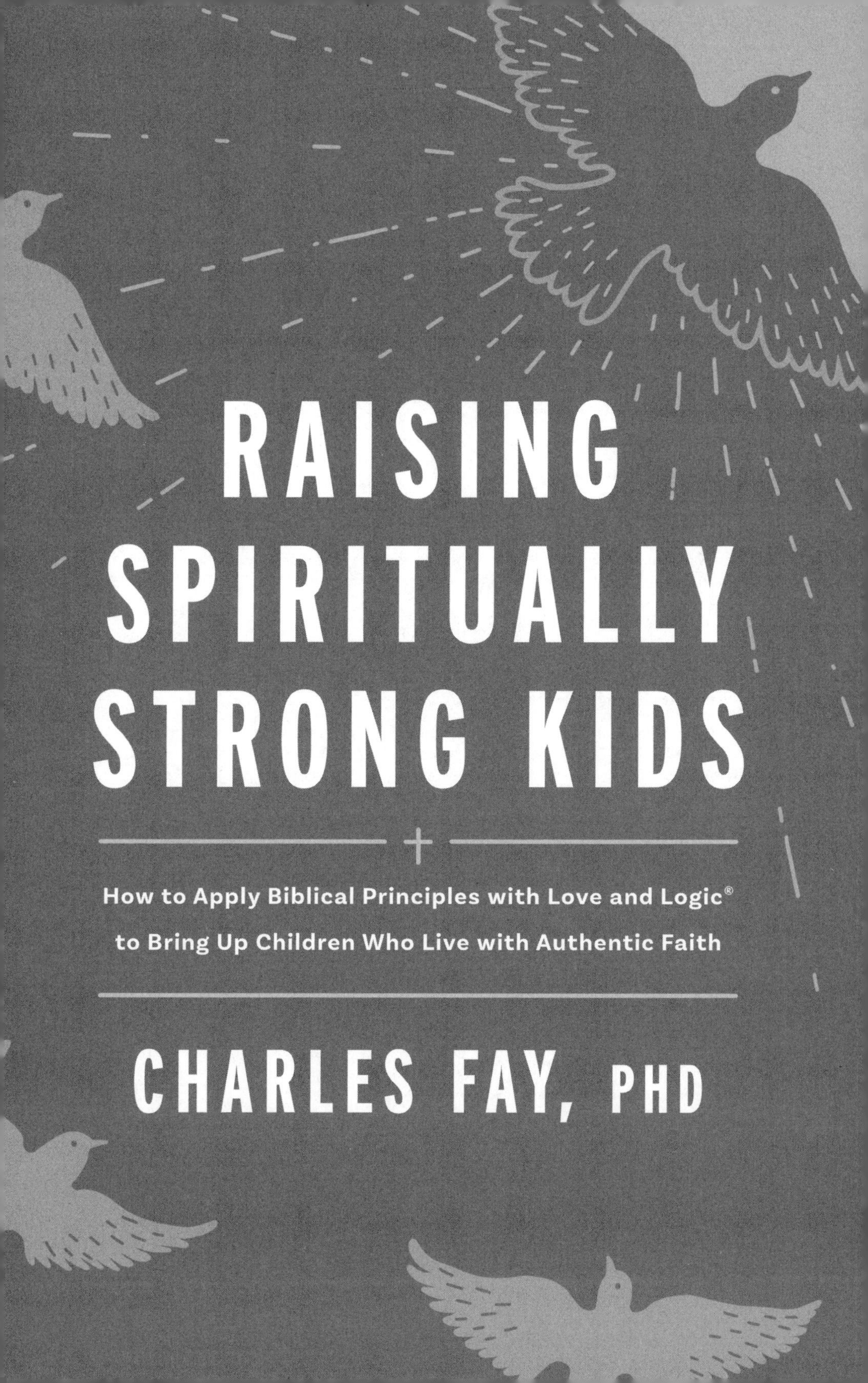

RAISING SPIRITUALLY STRONG KIDS

How to Apply Biblical Principles with Love and Logic® to Bring Up Children Who Live with Authentic Faith

CHARLES FAY, PHD

Visit Tyndale online at tyndale.com.

Tyndale, Tyndale's quill logo, *Tyndale Refresh*, and the Tyndale Refresh logo are are registered and/or common law trademarks of Tyndale House Ministries in the USA and various other jurisdictions around the world. All rights reserved. See tyndale.com for a full list of trademarks owned by Tyndale House Ministries. Tyndale Refresh is a nonfiction imprint of Tyndale House Publishers, Carol Stream, Illinois.

Raising Spiritually Strong Kids: How to Apply Biblical Principles with Love and Logic® to Bring Up Children Who Live with Authentic Faith

Cover design by Libby Dykstra

Interior design by Cathy Miller

The stories in this book are based on situations faced by families the author has worked with over several decades. Names and identifying details have been changed to protect people's privacy, and the dialogue reflects conversations the author has had with many clients.

For information about special discounts for bulk purchases, please contact Tyndale House Publishers at csresponse@tyndale.com, or call 1-855-277-9400.

Library of Congress Cataloging-in-Publication Data

A catalog record for this book is available from the Library of Congress.

ISBN 979-8-4005-1086-1

Printed in the United States of America

32 31 30 29 28 27 26
7 6 5 4 3 2 1

This book is dedicated to my Savior and Lord, Jesus Christ.

Dear Lord, I know that all good things come from You. Only in You do we find our hope, security, and salvation. Thank You for loving us so much that You paid the price for our sins and rose again to give us eternal life in You.

Only because of Your grace and Your power was I able to finish this book.

> Unless the LORD builds the house,
> those who build it labor in vain.
> Unless the LORD watches over the city,
> the watchman stays awake in vain.
>
> **PSALM 127:1**

CONTENTS

FOREWORD

When Dr. Charles Fay and I first began working together, we discovered something powerful and reassuring: The principles that help children become mentally strong—empathy paired with accountability; responsibility developed through experience; calm, loving leadership; and brain healthy habits—are deeply aligned with how God designed us to grow. Our collaboration on *Raising Mentally Strong Kids* was rooted in a shared conviction that children thrive when parents lead by example with both compassion and clarity.

This book takes that conviction to its deepest and most important place.

In *Raising Spiritually Strong Kids*, Dr. Fay expands the conversation beyond behavior, resilience, or emotional regulation and addresses the question that matters most to parents of faith: How do we help our children develop a genuine, lasting relationship with God—one that holds up when life gets hard?

What I admire most about this book is its honesty. Dr. Fay is clear that parents cannot control their children's faith. They cannot force belief, manufacture surrender, or prevent every struggle. And that truth, rather than being discouraging, is profoundly freeing. Parents are not called to be saviors; they are called to be faithful guides, reflecting God's love and strength in everyday moments.

As a psychiatrist and brain-health expert, I've seen how fear-based parenting undermines both emotional and spiritual growth. When parents operate from anxiety—rescuing too quickly, controlling too tightly, or striving for perfection—children may comply outwardly but struggle inwardly. Dr. Fay offers a better way: parenting that mirrors God's character by combining empathy with firm boundaries, grace with truth, and patience with responsibility.

This book gently dismantles the myth that spiritual strength comes from good behavior alone. Instead, it shows that faith matures when children are allowed to experience consequences, wrestle with choices, and discover over time that God is trustworthy. Discipline, when delivered with empathy, becomes a powerful teacher. Struggle, when supported but not removed, becomes a pathway to resilience and deeper belief.

Another strength of this book is its grace toward parents. Dr. Fay does not demand perfection. He understands that parents will make mistakes, lose patience, and sometimes get it wrong. Rather than shaming those moments, he reframes them as opportunities. When parents repair relationships, apologize sincerely, and model humility, children learn what faith looks like in real life—not in theory, but in practice.

We live in a world that constantly tells parents to shield children from discomfort and to equate love with protection from pain. This book offers a wiser, more hopeful truth: Children become spiritually strong, not by being rescued from every hardship, but by learning—through loving guidance—that God is present in the midst of it.

If you are a parent who wants more than outward obedience . . .

If you long to raise children who are emotionally grounded and spiritually anchored . . .

If you desire a home marked by peace, truth, and growing faith . . .

This book will serve you well.

Read it thoughtfully. Apply it imperfectly. Trust God consistently.

Because when parents reflect God's love *and* His strength, children don't just learn how to behave—they learn how to believe, persevere, and live with purpose.

Daniel G. Amen, MD

INTRODUCTION

PAINTING A PORTRAIT OF GOD'S STRENGTH AND LOVE

Since you've picked up this book, you're probably a parent whose faith is important to you—and who wants it to matter to your kids. In the midst of child-rearing, it feels *so* important to pass on your convictions. In fact, when it comes to your children's spiritual lives, getting this right can feel urgent. You may wonder how to guide a younger child's behavior and beliefs so they learn to follow God's voice as well as your own. If you have an older child, you want them to experience a dynamic life of faith—even when they've left the house and are making their own choices.

The stakes are high, and it may seem as though the deck is stacked against you and me: While there are some hopeful signs that the tide is turning, over the past few decades teens and young adults have left "institutional religion"—and often, their faith—in droves.[1] How do we ensure that our children are not part of that exodus? In a cynical world, how do we teach them to treat all people with kindness and respect?

In the pages of this book, you will learn how to help your kids draw closer to God as they also learn how to behave in respectful and considerate ways. You will discover how to do these things without fighting unwinnable control battles.

This was the same lesson I needed to learn as a young parent. One day when my oldest son was a toddler, I decided to give my wife a break and take him out for breakfast. At the time, I was still working my way through graduate studies in psychology. Not only was I reading in-depth research on different approaches to parenting, but my wife and I were also receiving tons of advice from friends and family.

The chaos began not long after our meal arrived. My son decided it was fun to scream at the top of his lungs and run away from me every time I asked him to return to the table. He put some egg into his mouth, but most of it quickly came right back out.

Of course, other patrons were looking our way. Trying my best to look in control, I quickly riffled through my mental filing cabinet of psychological theories and parenting strategies. Unfortunately, the thing was packed so full that I couldn't make sense of anything. Desperate to relieve my feelings of helplessness and embarrassment, I began lecturing my toddler about starving kids who would be thankful to have his food. I reminded him that money does not grow on trees and that it's important to show respect.

Needless to say, my son did not suddenly improve his behavior and proclaim, "I'm sorry, Dad. Now that you mention those facts, I realize that I need to acquire a better attitude." My arguments fell on deaf ears—in fact, his screaming only intensified as I was making them. Finally, I picked him up and raced out of the restaurant as quickly as I could—which was difficult since my son was squirming and screeching in protest.

Not only was I driven by my anxiety and desire to control my toddler, I was also stumbling over the falsehood that somehow I could ensure that my son would begin to grow spiritually if I could just get him to behave. What I often forgot was that good behavior is not synonymous with spiritual strength. Let me be clear: Teaching our kids how to act appropriately is extremely important, but it does not ensure that they will love God. The world is filled with well-behaved people who have no interest in Him.

My desire to do the right things, combined with the massive amount of information bouncing around in my head, had left me paralyzed. Fortunately, God had placed a wonderful person into our lives: Irma, our eighty-three-year-old next-door neighbor. After carefully listening as I shared what I viewed as a colossal parenting failure at the restaurant, she replied, "Oh, Charles, bringing up young'uns is not for the faint of heart. You are making it too complicated, and that's locking you up. If you can clear out your head a bit and remember two things, you'll be just fine."

"What are they?" I asked, listening intently.

Irma answered, "God is strong, and God is loving. He's the best parent there is. Be those two things for your boy, and chances are good it will go well."

Irma's advice seemed a bit simplistic at first, but I soon discovered that it was wise. If I relied on God rather than my ability to control how everything went, I no longer had to remember specific techniques but could simply do my best to be strong and loving. We'll unpack these terms in much greater detail as we go along, but here are simple definitions:

Love: God's love toward us is patient, kind, honest, faithful, and forgiving. We are imperfect humans, so our love will never match His, yet we are in the best position to reflect God's grace to our kids. We do this by delighting in them—for example, by offering lots of eye contact, smiles, and loving touch. We also do so by consistently helping them see the wonderful qualities and gifts that God has given them.

Strength: Because we love our kids and want the best for them, we establish and hold firm limits. This gives them the security they need, even when they make mistakes. We encourage them to develop problem-solving skills and allow them to deal with the natural consequences of their actions while offering appropriate support.

Once I set out to parent with love and strength, something interesting happened. The things I was learning about parenting, human behavior, and God's plan for our lives began to make far more sense. I found it easier to let go of any suggested strategy that was not consistent with His strength and love.

The parents who simply do their best to be loving and demonstrate strength by saying no when necessary end up raising better-adjusted kids than parents who obsess over being perfect.

About that time God gave me another gift. I began to see a theme in the many families I work with: The parents who simply do their best to be loving and demonstrate strength by saying no when necessary end up raising better-adjusted kids than parents who obsess over being perfect. From all these personal and professional experiences, I began to see that anxiety and perfectionism are often the greatest and most common impediments to success among conscientious parents. Fear truly is the enemy of love.

MOVING PAST PERFECTIONISM AND PERMISSIVENESS

To be sure, our increased anxiety and perfectionism today are understandable. Over the past few decades, the number of parenting experts, books and articles on parenting, and parent training programs has exploded. Wanting our children to have the best possible future, we seek these resources out with good intentions—and many of the ideas and skills they provide are very good. But as a result of the internet, access to these ideas and techniques has been placed at our fingertips twenty-four hours a day, seven days a week.

While largely unintended, this glut of information has led to three unfortunate trends:

- More than ever, parents feel overwhelmed and anxious by the amount of conflicting information.
- Parents worry that just about every misbehavior or struggle could be a sign of a serious problem. Because online sources often don't fully explain mental, developmental, neurological, or educational disorders, many parents have a misunderstanding of when a diagnosis is appropriate. They may become hypervigilant about their children's behaviors and be quick to label every misbehavior or tendency without doing the due diligence of getting a professional evaluation.
- Often parents believe that if they can master the information and skills provided by us "experts," all will go well with their kids. They buy into what I refer to as the parenting prosperity gospel, believing that if they work hard enough, they will be rewarded with a smooth parenting life and well-adjusted, well-behaved, and spiritually strong kids.

Too often we believe that we can ensure success if we are willing to work hard enough. The lie goes as follows: "Any problem can be prevented or quickly solved if you simply use the appropriate system, employ the right service, are inspired by the right podcast, or buy the correct product." More often than not, our attempts at control in parenting lead to our kids rebelling and us experiencing feelings of shame and defeat.

We may even unintentionally stunt their spiritual growth by too frequently rescuing them from struggles and telling them exactly what they must do. Being micromanaged leads many children to rely more on their parents than Christ. When parents dictate that their kids believe in Jesus and follow a rigid set of religious rules, their kids often find ways to rebel. Surprisingly, permissiveness can lead to the same result: When we try to keep our kids happy all the time so they will like us, our limits are weak or nonexistent, and children may begin to see themselves as the center of everything with little need for God.

From One Parent to Another

So what do we do? Before we go further, it may help you to learn a bit more about my background and how it's influenced my understanding of why love and strength are the cornerstones of raising kids. My wife, Monica, and I are the parents of three sons who have given us plenty of hands-on experience. I also lead the Love and Logic Institute, an organization cofounded by my father, Jim Fay, an educational consultant, and child psychiatrist Foster Cline. For nearly fifty years, the Love and Logic Institute has taught parents how to combine empathy and accountability to build strong relationships with kids and help them become responsible, resilient, and respectful adults.

You should know one other thing about me. As a Christian, my faith is the driving force in my life. It would be impossible for me to write a book about raising spiritually strong kids from anything other than a Christian perspective. So while many of the practical tools offered in this book can be helpful in building strong character apart from faith, the principles are rooted in Scripture and the example and teachings of Jesus. To understand what virtues are and why character matters, it's helpful to reflect upon one simple fact repeatedly addressed in Scripture: God cares about more than our behavior. He is also passionately concerned with our habitual, heart-level attitudes and motivations.

I will be drawing on these principles throughout this book and also suggesting tools from the Love and Logic approach to parenting.

Along the way, many readers will recognize the degree to which the Love and Logic approach is rooted in biblical principles.

As we begin our journey, let's accurately and clearly define the term *spiritual strength*. Very concisely, it can be understood as a gift from God, characterized by continuous growth in the following tenets and characteristics:

- belief that God is the sovereign, good, and loving Creator and sustainer of all things
- awareness and hatred of the sin that so easily creeps into our lives, along with the recognition that only Jesus Christ can save us from the eternal consequences of sin and evil
- love toward God for what He has done in our lives
- desire to point others toward God by obeying His commandments and demonstrating His love through our thoughts and actions
- a trusting reliance on God, particularly in times of distress

I want to be clear: Our children develop spiritual strength only as they *personally* discover that they need the strength and love of Jesus Christ. Because of the choices they make, this transformation doesn't always happen as quickly or smoothly as we'd like. Even so, this beautiful dependency grows best when they feel His love and the security of His strength in the face of daily challenges. With this experience comes hope and heightened curiosity. Children curious about Jesus seek more of Him. We don't need to force them to follow Him because they run toward Him, drawn closer by His grace.

Our children develop spiritual strength only as they *personally* discover that they need the strength and love of Jesus Christ.

Since our children ultimately discover the love of Christ as a result of His grace, what does our role look like? As we'll see in part 1, once we accept that we don't have ultimate control over our kids' spiritual development, we can better steward the responsibility He has given us as parents. The critical first steps actually start with us, which is why we'll begin by discovering why aligning our own thoughts and values with God's is so important. Then we'll consider the various parenting styles that are often behind the approach we take in guiding our kids. Recognizing our default style enables us to choose a different way when it's called for.

With this newfound knowledge about ourselves, we'll explore the best ways to teach our kids to love God and others. This includes treating them with love and dignity, setting limits that lead to respect, and teaching them to accept responsibility for their actions. As you read, you will notice that I provide solutions to many of the daily challenges we face as parents. I do so because I know that parents are always blessed with those practical answers. More importantly, I offer them because God uses such trials to mature our faith—and that of our children.

As parents, we are artists. Moment by moment, day by day, and year by year we paint for our children a mental and emotional portrait of God and what it means to depend upon Him. Obviously, the fewer distortions, the better! The clearer and truer the picture is, the easier it will be for our children to recognize the true God and surrender their lives to Him. We can create this portrait of God as we go about our daily parenting business. How we handle skinned knees, picky eating, temper tantrums, whining about being bored, rushing to practice and games, disappointment over grades, troubling friendships, sibling spats, and every other parenting challenge can teach them about God and His ways. How we navigate challenges will have an important impact on our children's spiritual maturity and our own. We can choose to handle these with the weak and often changing principles of this world, or we can choose to rely on God's strength and the timeless wisdom He provides.

In part 2, I move from the basics toward concepts and strategies you can use to help guide your children toward maturity. These chapters provide biblically based solutions to common challenges, including how to help your kids

- develop attitudes of generosity and contentment rather than entitlement;
- build perseverance and problem-solving skills;
- become motivated to work hard in school and life;
- make healthy decisions about technology and social media; and
- navigate other dilemmas that frequently stump parents.

As gratifying as it is to see your kids mature and make good decisions, seeing your kids become spiritually strong is likely even more important to you. That's why, in the final chapter, you'll be encouraged to consider how you can help your kids learn to lean on God's ways rather than the fads and falsehoods offered by this world.

This book is packed with practical strategies for helping your children understand God's amazing love for them by seeing it in your actions toward them and experiencing a heartfelt awareness of their need for Christ. By living out these truths in your daily walk with them, you provide a picture of faith that is completely authentic and integrated into real life experience. You help them become committed and curious for Christ.

Regardless of your unique story, there is a place for you in the pages of this book. Maybe you are a parent of young children, wondering where you will find the energy and patience to make it through. Perhaps your children are older and you're hurting over the direction a child has already taken. Maybe you are in pain over how you were parented and fear that you will transmit what you see as family dysfunction to your own kids. Perhaps you are a stepparent, adoptive parent, or a grandparent who doesn't feel up to the task. Maybe you are single and finding it hard to make ends meet while devoting enough time and energy to your kids. The variety of life situations and struggles is too long to list, but God can handle them all. No matter your situation, it's okay to enjoy your kids and let each of them grow according to God's plan for their lives. It's okay to relax and let go of the very natural but counterproductive desire to make sure your kids always believe and do the right things. In the process of letting go, it is essential to remember that God is in control, and it is only through His grace that any of us, including our children, come to Him and grow in spiritual strength.

So as you read this book, please keep in mind that God is intensely and passionately devoted to helping you raise your children. You are not alone. When you become a Christian, His Spirit lives inside you!

PART 1

IT STARTS WITH US

The Basics of Raising Spiritually Strong Kids

CHAPTER 1

PARTNERS IN THE PROCESS

Our Role and Responsibility as Parents

One pleasant spring day my wife and I drove with our thirteen-year-old son to his baseball game. Just as I pulled into a parking spot at the ball field, my son yelled, "Dad! Did you put my cleats in the car? I can't find them! Why didn't you remind me?"

"What?" I barked, turning to glare at him. "It's not my job to gather your things! For crying out loud! How many times do I have to tell you to be more responsible about getting prepared for your games?"

Immediately, I felt remorse as my own words came back to haunt me. Just the day before, I'd spent two hours teaching a church group about the Love and Logic principles for parenting. At one point, I'd quoted Proverbs 15:1: "A gentle answer turns away wrath, but a harsh word stirs up anger" (NIV). I even brought up Ephesians 6:4, emphasizing that we should not provoke our children to anger but rather "bring them up in the training and instruction of the Lord"

(NIV). The entire gist of my talk revolved around the importance of moms and dads keeping their cool and calmly allowing natural consequences to do the teaching.

Of course, my not-so-gentle answer at the ballpark stirred up plenty of anger and drama, leaving me feeling like a horrible father and a spiritual hypocrite. Yes, it was my son's responsibility to remember what he needed for the game. He was now a teenager after all. But my attitude about the whole thing stunk. I'd lost my cool, and the way I handled the situation was neither strong nor loving.

Racked with guilt, I drove home and retrieved his cleats while he warmed up for the game. So much for painting a picture of God's strength and love.

As I lay in bed that night, my mind raced once again as I thought about the horrible example I had set. Had I ruined my son's chances of developing the spiritual values and faith I hoped to pass along? Would he grow up to be short-tempered and irresponsible?

OUR TRUE RESPONSIBILITY

If you've ever had an experience like that, you are not alone. We all make mistakes. We all have days when our actions and words don't match the way we want to parent. Our pain and anxiety are elevated because the stakes seem exceedingly high. If our kids end up rejecting God, will it be our fault?

As a child psychologist, I am often asked questions such as "How do I get my kids to do their chores?" or "How do I get them excited about learning at school?" Although these questions may seem irrelevant to spiritual matters, the way we handle them is not. It is true that how we treat our kids is often more influential than what we say to them. Even the smallest interaction is an opportunity to show our children, whether through the tone

> We have great influence over our kids' spiritual development, but we do not have ultimate control.

of our voice or the way we treat others, that following God brings us hope and strength.

Yet before we go any further, I need to remind you of something I pointed out in the introduction: The entirety of our kids' spiritual development does not rest on our shoulders. We have great influence, but we do not have ultimate control. This is good news!

The Bible instructs us to set our sights on heaven above, letting go of trying to control what we cannot: "Think about the things of heaven, not the things of earth" (Colossians 3:2, NLT). The apostle Paul goes on to show how that mindset affects the way we live (and parent):

> Clothe yourselves with tenderhearted mercy, kindness, humility, gentleness, and patience. Make allowance for each other's faults, and forgive anyone who offends you. . . . Above all, clothe yourselves with love, which binds us all together in perfect harmony. And let the peace that comes from Christ rule in your hearts.
>
> **COLOSSIANS 3:12-15, NLT**

Paul offers no guarantee that other people—including our kids—will reciprocate, but regardless, we can have peace when we follow God's ways. Our responsibility is *not* to ensure the outcome; we simply can't determine whether or not our children ultimately choose to follow Christ. What we *can* control are our own actions and commitment to God and His commandments.

Christ summed this up clearly and beautifully:

> You shall love the Lord your God with all your heart and with all your soul and with all your mind. This is the great and first commandment. And a second is like it:

> You shall love your neighbor as yourself. On these two commandments depend all the Law and the Prophets.
> MATTHEW 22:37-40

Loving and trusting Jesus gives us the spiritual power required to love others, including ourselves. Such love both originates in and is refined by Him.[1] Only in this intimate relationship with Him can we truly succeed. Jesus is not only the author and perfecter of *our* faith, but also of our *children*'s.[2] So then how should we approach issues of faith with them? What parts of their faith journey are our responsibility? If we intend to raise spiritually strong children, we must continually wrestle with these challenging questions.

Of course, seeking God in His Word and through prayer is always the first step.

We might also look at how Charles Spurgeon, a prominent nineteenth-century pastor and theologian, explains the way steadfast faith in Christ develops so that we may further parse out what is within our control as parents and what is only within the purview of God. The terms he uses may sound a bit formal and even outdated to us, but stick with me: I think they succinctly summarize the steps we and our kids take on the way to true spiritual strength.[3]

Knowledge. Spurgeon asserts what is obvious: It's impossible for anyone to develop a strong faith in God if they are not told about Him. This is definitely within our control and is our responsibility. We must help our children get to know Him and His commandments. We teach our children about spiritual matters by weaving God's Word into all that we do and say:

> You must love the LORD your God with all your heart, all your soul, and all your strength. And you must commit yourselves wholeheartedly to these commands that I am

> giving you today. Repeat them again and again to your children. Talk about them when you are at home and when you are on the road, when you are going to bed and when you are getting up. Tie them to your hands and wear them on your forehead as reminders. Write them on the doorposts of your house and on your gates.
>
> **DEUTERONOMY 6:5-9,** NLT

You teach God's ways as you model your undivided love for Him, read the Bible to your children, encourage them to learn about Him from others, and demonstrate His love and power through effective discipline. As you come to know God better, it will feel more natural to point your children to the Creator in daily life; for instance, when you walk together outside or sing along to a praise song when you and your kids are in the car. Specifically, what might this look like for parents who are able to start when their children are very young?

At three years old, little Candace didn't understand the deep theological implications of the Lord's Prayer, but after reading her a bedtime story, her parents prayed Matthew 6:9-13 with her just about every evening. In the process, she heard many truths: We have a Father in heaven who created everything and is worthy of great respect and praise because He is our King; He gives us what we need each day; He is loving and forgiving; He wants us to be loving and forgiving toward others; and He is our protector.

Almost every day, Candy's parents also pointed out the good things—from strawberries to sunshine to Sasha their dog—that God made and provides for our benefit. They did their best to show her what forgiveness looks like by modeling grace in their marriage and their relationships with others, as well as in the way they disciplined her. They continued to pray as a family for others, for themselves, and for the wisdom to remember to put God first.

Before she entered elementary school, Candy knew that all of us sin (see Romans 3:23) and that the consequences of this sin are eternal doom and suffering (see Romans 6:23). She also knew the good news that God loves us so much that He gave His only Son to die for our sins (see John 3:16).

Of course, by the time Candy entered adolescence, she'd heard many more truths from the Bible. Her parents had taught her how to use God's Word to guide her prayer life and her choices. Just as important, she continued to see her parents, as well as other adults close to her, seek to live godly lives. As a result, her knowledge of God and His good news was not only based on what she'd been told and what she had read, but also on what she had seen and how she was treated.

If your children are older, and you haven't started sharing God's truth with them, it is never too late to start. Regardless of their age or stage in life, don't underestimate the power of allowing them to witness your joy over the good and beautiful things God has placed in your life. The more often they see and hear your praise and joy, the more seeds of faith you help plant in their minds. Of course, their experience of your love for them and your thankfulness to God for bringing them into your life, is the most vital of such "thankfulness seeds." While this can be difficult with a sullen, argumentative teen, never underestimate its power. Over time, such love and gratitude is one of the many ways that God uses parents to plant knowledge of Himself in the minds of their children.

As our kids grow older, the hardships we face can also go a long way toward helping them develop in their knowledge of God. Of course, this is the case only when they see us trusting in His strength to see us through. It is quite humbling, indeed, to consider the fact that God may be allowing trials in our lives for the purpose of helping others see that He gives comfort beyond understanding.

Regardless of a child's age, it is helpful to share Scripture that has helped you address conflicts with others, times of disappointment, anxieties, temptations, or other challenges. Doing so has two benefits. The first and most obvious is that it shows that God's truth helps you in your times of need; second, it demonstrates your humility. From the beginning, God has used humble people in powerful ways to share His timeless truth. Because faith is a gift from Him and Him alone, this does not guarantee that your kids will accept His gracious gift of salvation. Regardless of the outcome, you will know that you have been faithful and that God is in control.

Assent. The second requirement in the development of faith, according to Spurgeon, is assent: More than knowing the gospel message, we put full confidence in the Scriptures and agree that Christ is the only Lord and Savior. As Spurgeon says, "You are not allowed to halve the Scriptures, and to believe what you please; you are not allowed to believe the Scripture with a half-heartedness, for if you do this wilfully, you have not the faith which looks alone to Christ."[4]

This step is where our control ends and God's begins. Now certainly as we've discussed, we can provide a picture of what this acceptance looks like in our own daily walk. We can teach our kids about it. We can bring them to church and encourage them to learn from other godly people. We can emulate God's strength and grace in the way we discipline. We can demonstrate joy and the other fruit of the Spirit in our attitudes and behaviors toward others. All these actions fall within our control and responsibility.

We cannot, however, place belief and agreement into their hearts. Only God can do this.

God commands us to share the truth of His Word in what we say and do. He does not hold us responsible for what our children, or anyone else, choose to do with what we have shared.

Consider Laura's story. She adored her twenty-three-year-old daughter, Bethany, but the power struggles they'd had over the young woman's lifestyle choices were wearing Laura down. Laura's feelings of shame mingled with anger, anxiety, and fear. Although an incredibly bright and dynamic child, Bethany tested every limit and seemed to revel in saying no to almost everything her mother asked her to do. By the time she left home at age nineteen, she'd experimented with almost everything she had been taught was wrong.

Laura told me about her pain, but she also said that God was giving her a sense of peace in the midst of this turmoil. "While praying one morning, it came to me that I had done everything I could to teach Bethany about God. I had taken her to church, gotten her involved in Bible study groups, and tried to help her understand the gospel by living out my faith. I wasn't a perfect parent, but I always tried to treat her like Jesus has treated me.

"It also came to me that I didn't have to feel guilty or angry about the choices she was making. These were *her* choices, and they were about her life and her relationship with God, not mine," Laura said.

Understanding that only God can lead someone to accept His Word freed Laura from her pain and self-condemnation. "It helped me see that my shame was keeping me from having closeness with God *and* a relationship with my daughter," Laura said. "This pain was leading me to believe that I had to control her even more. It's crazy. I spent a lot of time feeling like I'd be letting down God if I didn't constantly point out her bad choices and lecture her about them."

"That's a heavy load to carry," I commented.

"Backbreaking!" Laura agreed. "I still worry about her almost all the time, but now I can enjoy her and love her. I realized that I don't have to fight with her about her choices, because I have already shared God's truth with her. I can now focus on other things within my control like whether I show her how much I love her, enjoy the times we have together, have good boundaries, and pray without ceasing. Only God can change her heart."

Affiance. Spurgeon uses this old-fashioned word to sum up the critical step of coming to true faith, which he says is "not the believing it merely, but the taking hold of it as being ours, and in the resting on it for salvation."[5] In this word you might see the more familiar word *fiancé*, which is derived from this very old and rarely used one. Of course, a fiancé is given in marriage, an act of absolute and very intimate devotion, oneness, and faithfulness, to another. Likewise, solid faith reaches full maturity when we become one with Christ. The concept of affiance implies the closeness, devotion, and trust that goes beyond just knowing and agreeing that Christ is the Lord and Savior of the universe. It is giving our all to Him.

Just as we can't simply reason our way to a lifelong love for a potential spouse, we can't think our way to a deep and permanent commitment to Christ. Knowing about Him can remain a distant and purely intellectual exercise. Knowing Him intimately is evidence of a new heart. Those with affiance act in obedience to His commands and proclaim through their words and behavior, "Praise Jesus! He is mine and I am His. We are one. He is my *personal* Lord and Savior!"

Similar to the previous stage of spiritual development, whether or not our children attain affiance with Christ is ultimately outside of our control. However, while Christ is the author and perfecter of our children's faith, it *is* within our power and duty to cooperate with the process; and though it can be uncomfortable to acknowledge, true affiance comes through a measure of disruption. After all, true trust develops through trials. By allowing our children to encounter age-appropriate struggles without needlessly rescuing them, we are giving them opportunities to grow in their spiritual strength, to deepen their connection with their Savior.

Operating like helicopters on high-stakes search and rescue missions, far too many parents constantly hover over their kids, micromanage their actions, rescue them from their poor choices, and generally do everything they can to create an adversity-free life. As a result, their children never discover that they can cope with hardship.

A strong body of research demonstrates the link between chronic helicopter parenting and mental illness in youth.[6] Instead of understanding that trials are part of life and good for learning, these kids view them as causes for extreme panic or despair. Few things breed anxiety, fear, depression, and entitlement more than this! From a spiritual perspective, those who are too often protected from growth by being rescued from difficulties may not come to know God as their "refuge and strength" (Psalm 46:1).

Of course, it's not always easy to watch our kids struggle when we could step in and make their situations easier. Steve discovered this when his daughter Emma felt serious discomfort in her college biology course. She'd spent too much time procrastinating to complete all her homework and adequately study for the exams. To make matters worse, her professor was a stickler for details and showed little or no mercy to his students. It was clear he was not about to give Emma a passing grade, even though she had very politely and respectfully asked him if he'd allow her to earn some extra credit. She felt crushed. Retaking the class seemed like her only option—unless she could get her dad to put some pressure on the university.

"This professor just doesn't understand how difficult the content is," she told Steve over the phone. "He assigns way too much work on the lab assignments, and he counts off for even the smallest mistakes."

Emma's dad empathized. "That does sound tough. I can tell that you are hurting over this."

Emma pleaded, "I don't need very many points to pass, and I was wondering if you could email the dean of students. Maybe he would listen to you."

Hurting for his daughter but knowing that she needed to experience this struggle, Steve answered, "I could do that, but I don't think it would be the best thing for you in the long run. I believe in you, Emma, and I know you can work this out. Would you like to discuss some ideas?"

Disappointed, Emma answered, "I guess I just have to retake the class."

When in a spirit of firmness and love we allow our kids to face some of life's inevitable struggles, we give them the opportunity to see that Christ is the God of all comfort. They can rely on Him to guide them through life's difficulties, and when they look to Him, they grow in emotional maturity and faith.

As we consider the basic process by which God matures us spiritually, it's important to remember that He controls the timing, initiation, and trajectory. For some people, growth happens early and in a steady, linear fashion. For others it may start later or progress in what we believe is an unpredictable, haphazard, and "messy" way. Still others don't seem to grow at all. Again, it is important to remember that the only thing within our control is how well we teach and model God's truth. No good can possibly come from us worrying that our children are not growing quickly or smoothly enough. Likewise, there is no benefit in taking pride in how seamlessly we believe they are progressing.

A STRONG AND LOVING MODEL

Once we understand the general trajectory of spiritual development—from knowledge to assent to affiance—we can better answer the question: What's *our* particular responsibility in helping our kids develop a solid faith relationship with Jesus Christ?

As we've seen, our role is to share Him and to model His love. But that means if we want to be the most effective in raising spiritually strong children, we must also confront and assess our *own* spiritual strength. Do we bask in God's love, or do we constantly strive to control our lives in an attempt to meet our own needs? Do we choose to worship Him as our only God, or do we also look for hope in idols such as wealth, comfort, personal accomplishment, or even our relationship with our kids?

Q & A: What Should You Do When You Disagree with Your Spouse (or Former Spouse) About a Parenting Issue?

You and your spouse may agree that you want to help your children learn to love God and rely on His strength, only to discover that you have very different ideas on how to do that. While disagreement between parents is common, it's important to keep it from morphing into extreme conflict. When anger and dissension simmer, kids can develop long-term problems like anxiety, anger, depression, shame, and the adoption of unhealthy coping strategies, all of which make it more difficult for them to enjoy healthy adult relationships. Here are some quick suggestions on how to navigate conflict between parents.

- **Remember that power struggles achieve horrible results.** Many people make the mistake of believing that if they constantly nag, remind, criticize, or otherwise pressure someone into seeing their point of view, that person will suddenly see the light and wholeheartedly comply. Truth be told, these methods either result in overt conflict or passive resistance, depending on the personality of the one who feels controlled. Either way, children suffer.

- **Let go of the belief that there is only one way to achieve a desired result.** This isn't easy, which is why couples must first identify and agree upon their foundational parenting values. Examples include:

    - We will do our best to always act in ways consistent with loving God and loving others.
    - We will show our children what cooperation, respect, love, and grace look like in a marriage.
    - We will demonstrate unconditional love toward them, while setting firm limits.
    - We will allow our children to make plenty of affordable mistakes.
    - We will allow them to face the natural consequences of their mistakes without needlessly rescuing them.

- When we disagree about how to parent, we will pray together and seek God's help in doing what brings honor to Him so that our children can see what His love looks like.

Once we identify our shared values, we can let go of trying to control others by supporting them as they handle issues and situations in ways that may differ from how we would.

- **Place most of our focus on our own attitudes and behavior.** Most of what we are taught in the Bible addresses *our own* relationship with God and *our own* attitudes and actions toward others. When Scripture does address our responsibility to correct others, it emphasizes that we are to do so with an attitude of humility and love. Our influence on the attitudes and actions of others, including our spouses and children, depends far more on our daily walk than our talk.

- **Remember that few things are more ineffective than criticism.** Perhaps the most dangerous and destructive form of disagreement is faultfinding. Often it's meant as constructive feedback, but it is provided far too often and in the absence of encouragement. Expressing thankfulness toward the other parent, and focusing on their strengths, is one of the best gifts we can give our children. They desperately need to see that their parents love and respect each other.

Pause and let the awareness of God's love sink in. How much does God love you? How often do you spend time thinking about the depth of His adoration for you? How frequently do you consider the awesome fact that He, the Creator and sustainer of the universe, knows everything about you and delights in you as His precious child? You are able to love because you accept the truth that God first loved you. Focusing on this will allow you to best love your kids in ways that help them grow stronger in every way.

As we discussed in the last section, true love means doing what's best for our children's long-term spiritual welfare, even though sometimes that means acting in ways that allow our children to face discomfort. Love doesn't mean always being lenient. As we know, God is love, but He is not permissive. After all, to assist in our own spiritual development, doesn't God set limits with us? When we choose to go our own way, does He always swoop in to save us from the consequences? It's true that God allows us to experience the natural, sometimes painful outcomes of our actions—and He is always ready to offer His comfort and guidance when we turn back to Him.

We are called to do the same for our kids. We love them while also holding them accountable for their actions. Rather than constantly jumping through hoops to ensure their comfort, we prioritize the development of their character through growth and struggle. Out of His incomprehensible love, God allows us to encounter the full range of life experience, from happiness and delight to discouragement and fear. He does so to draw us to Him and show us that we can experience joy, peace, and contentment only through a faithful relationship with Him. Our responsibility as parents is to not interfere with this process in the lives of our children.

As Christians, the Holy Spirit lives within us, prompting and empowering us to see, enjoy, and obey God in everything, including parenting. This doesn't mean it's easy or even natural for many of us to follow God's leading, particularly during times of discouragement, fear, or anger. This has definitely been a challenge for me! The more we listen and obey, however, the more effective we will be as we guide our kids.

Consistently providing a true picture of God's love is challenging to say the least! Because of this, we must rely on God to show us when to act versus when to be still and trust. And when we fail, we can be sure He will lift us up: "The LORD is like a father to his children, tender and compassionate to those who fear him. For he knows how weak we are; he remembers we are only dust" (Psalm 103:13-14, NLT).

PERFECTION NOT REQUIRED

You and I are in good company. The Bible is packed with examples of imperfect people, both men and women, who recognized their frailties and looked to God for wisdom and strength. Perhaps the greatest requirement for success in parenting is the recognition of God's love for us despite our flaws. There is perfect purpose even in our imperfection. Who better to show our children, who are also imperfect, that God performs His greatest miracles when we acknowledge our weakness in the face of seemingly overwhelming challenges? The pattern is well-established in Scripture: God loved His children so much that He parted the Red Sea so that they could escape the formidable power of Pharaoh and his army. He loved His children so much that He fed a huge number of them, five thousand, with only five loaves of bread and two fish. He loves us so much that He gave His only Son to rescue us from the overwhelming power of sin and death. From these examples and many others, we see that God is all-powerful. He deserves our worship.

Perhaps the greatest requirement for success in parenting is the recognition of God's love for us despite our flaws.

We also experience hope that He will empower us through immense tasks such as parenting.

The Bible outlines the story of God's flawed and rebellious children and the hope He provides for redemption and restoration. We are those children. All of us are deeply loved prodigals raising prodigals utterly dependent upon the grace of God. His power is made perfect in our weakness. In this humble state we are best positioned to point our children toward the strength, love, and contentment that comes only through a personal relationship with Christ.

In fact, one of the beautiful benefits of building a deep relationship with God is the wisdom He provides during the process. As the apostle John says, "Whoever confesses that Jesus is the Son of God, God abides in him, and he in God. So we have come to know and to *believe* the love that God has for us" (1 John 4:15-16, emphasis added). Nurturing our own spiritual growth is not always easy. In fact, sometimes it feels like an impossible struggle to live out the strength and love God has shown us. God is graceful. As we seek Him, He will not leave us unchanged.

Fortunately, our kids tend to be understanding toward us as well. When I blew it with my son by yelling at him for forgetting his baseball cleats, God used my deep regret to help me see that my anger stemmed from the belief that I always had to be the "hero" by making sure everything went okay.

The next day I confessed this to my son and apologized for letting my frustration get the best of me. After I said how sorry I was, he hugged me and said, "It's okay, Dad. It's like you always say: 'You don't have to be perfect.'"

In the chapters to come, I will help you reconsider the long-held beliefs that drive how you think and respond to your kids too. Doing so won't make you perfect, but it will enable you to parent with greater intention and peace—keys to raising spiritually strong kids.

CHAPTER 2

THE WISEST WAY

Using God's Truth to Direct Our Parenting

Three parents sip coffee and huddle in a circle during a break at a parenting seminar. They came highly motivated to be the very best parents they could be, but each had been hitting some setbacks.

"I don't know why I have such a hard time breaking these bad habits! I don't want to yell," says Louise, "but it seems like my mother's words come out of my mouth anytime I have to discipline my kids."

Taylor nods. "I know what you mean! My parents didn't yell, but they made me feel bad with lots of guilt trips," he says. "The other day I found myself sounding just like my dad, asking my son, 'After all that I do for you, this is the way you treat me?' It makes me sick to admit it."

"My parents were always so legalistic," Jose laments. "I never felt like my brother and I could have any fun. Now I'm realizing that I go to the other extreme with my kids. I've been way too permissive, and now their behavior is really showing it."

Perhaps the biggest challenge in parenting has very little to do with the kids in our homes but the ones in our heads. These "kids" are the beliefs and ideas we were raised with, as well as the ones we adopt and choose to dwell on as adults. When we take time to stop and examine them, we may be surprised to discover that they drive us to respond to our children in ways that are at odds with our love for Christ and for them.

Simply put, our deepest beliefs impact how we parent, and how we parent impacts what our children will come to believe. If what they believe becomes the filter through which they interpret everything—ultimately determining how they choose to think, feel, and act—then our work is to help them develop a truth-oriented filter. This will dramatically increase the odds that they will move in the direction of healthy spiritual growth rather than being led astray by the ever-changing philosophical winds of this world. We are best positioned to do that work when we first begin to confront what *we* truly believe.

> Our deepest beliefs impact how we parent, and how we parent impacts what our children will come to believe.

Before we move forward, it's important to emphasize what I mean by a "truth-oriented filter." To be clear, the truth I am talking about is God's truth as revealed in His Word, the Bible, not our culture or our own personal desires. Reflecting the character of God, the Word of God is eternal, unchanging, life-giving, grace-filled, and powerful beyond our comprehension. God's character does not always leave us feeling comfortable, but His truths will always move us toward greater godliness and peace.

RETHINKING OUR PRIORITIES AS PARENTS

A belief that many conscientious, loving parents hold is that "good" parents make sure their kids are both happy and well-behaved. When

I ask people what they want for their kids, most include these two characteristics at the top of their list. Certainly my wife, Monica, and I have always wanted our boys to be happy and well-mannered. Both desires are normal and good as long as they are not elevated above our children having their own relationship with Jesus Christ.

Let's first consider whether the priority of happiness passes the truth-oriented filter. Have you ever noticed that the apostle Paul never mentions it as one of the signs that God is at work in our lives?

> The fruit of the Spirit is love, joy, peace, patience,
> kindness, goodness, faithfulness, gentleness, self-control;
> against such things there is no law.
>
> **GALATIANS 5:22-23**

Notice that joy makes the list, but happiness does not. Why? From a Christian standpoint, joy is God-centered. It comes from God and our relationship with Him, and it brings glory to Him. Unlike happiness, it is not dependent upon fulfilled desires or favorable circumstances.

If we are parenting our children to be spiritually strong, happiness cannot be our main priority; after all, teaching our children to dwell on what is true will not always make them happy. In fact, the more faithful they are to God, the more opposition they will face from others who are doing wrong. They will also experience discomfort when they stray from what they know is right.

At the age of ten, Marcus, a dear friend of mine, felt the tug of God on his heart and committed his life to Christ. He had the great benefit of having parents who believed that doing what is right is far more important than doing what makes one temporarily happy. His dad once told him that one of his favorite verses was "I would rather be a gatekeeper in the house of my God than live the good life in the homes of the wicked" (Psalm 84:10, NLT). During elementary school, he experienced relatively little pushback over his Christian values. This changed as Marcus neared adolescence. By middle and high school, he took a great deal of flak for avoiding pornography, violent videos, and angry music. He was teased because he didn't make a practice of swearing or telling dirty jokes.

Like any kid, Marcus wanted to be happy and accepted by his most popular peers. One day this desire finally led him to join in with a group of boys as they joked, laughed, and talked in great detail about some very inappropriate things. Much to Marcus's surprise, this did not make him happy. Instead, he felt only great anxiety and regret afterward.

Marcus is now a godly father of three children. He is a generally happy man, not because he was taught to pursue it but because God changed his heart to feel the greatest joy when he was doing what pleased God.

God wants something far better for our children than merely the pursuit of happiness. Could it be that service, sacrifice, and honoring Him bring greater and more enduring blessings?[1]

Focusing on this truth enables us to build our spiritual house upon solid rock rather than shifting sand:

> Everyone then who hears these words of mine and does them will be like a wise man who built his house on the rock. And the rain fell, and the floods came, and the winds blew and beat on that house, but it did not fall, because it had been founded on the rock. And everyone who hears these words of mine and does not do them will be like a foolish man who built his house on the sand. And the rain fell, and the floods came, and the winds blew and beat against that house, and it fell, and great was the fall of it.
>
> **MATTHEW 7:24-27**

We will never regret teaching our children to pursue and serve God rather than their personal comfort or happiness. This perspective will never let them down, even when the storms of life come their way. When they learn to focus on seeking His truth, He will reveal the best ways for them to think and live. Although they will still face some strong winds, rain, and rising waters, they won't have to live in constant anxiety, fear, or despair. They can experience joy.

Now let's consider the belief that raising well-behaved kids will cause them to become spiritually strong and right with God. Does this notion really pass the truth test? No. The Bible is clear: No one can earn entrance into heaven with even the very best conduct. We are saved by grace through faith in Jesus Christ (see Ephesians 2:8-9). Politeness, kindness, and other positive behaviors are good, but they can't meet God's holy standard. They have no power to save anyone from eternal suffering and separation from God (see Isaiah 64:6).

Even those parents who understand this may become so committed to promoting righteous behavior in their children that they fail to show them that Christianity centers on a faith relationship with Christ, not on following rules. I bring this up because much of this book is devoted to strategies for teaching good behavior. We discover that this is not a contradiction when we remember that faith without works is dead (see James 2:26). God is the sole architect of our faith and our children's faith. He does, however, command us to grow in good habits that demonstrate our love for Him and for others.

Being happy and polite will not protect our children from picking up the lies that show up everywhere in our culture—whether it's the false belief that their value comes from outward appearance or excellence in athletics, academics, or other endeavors, or the idea that they are free to think and be whatever they want. What does provide spiritual protection is steeping them in God's love and truth found in a relationship with Him and the words of the Bible.

Accomplishing this doesn't have to be complicated, and it doesn't require a seminary degree. Certainly it doesn't involve constantly pointing out to our children what we think they are doing wrong. Instead, teaching God's truth should be a natural outcome of seeking to know and apply His truth in our own walk with Him. As we do, we will begin to grow beyond the many beliefs and thoughts that can sabotage our parenting skills. We'll also begin to understand how best to share the pursuit of truth with our children in authentic and easily understandable ways.

GOING FIRST

Very generally, there are two types of teachers: those who know what they are teaching, and those who not only know the material but have also consumed it so deeply that it has become part of them. Shortly after God called Ezekiel, the prophet was given a scroll containing God's message to the nation of Israel and told: "Son of man, eat what is before you, eat this scroll; then go and speak to the people of Israel" (Ezekiel 3:1, NIV).

The message he received was so important that Ezekiel needed to consume it. Since it's so essential to educate our children on the importance of focusing on truth, we are wise to begin integrating God's instruction into our own lives first. We can then speak patiently from deep personal understanding while also providing compelling examples from our own experience.

How do we do this? I want to share three important steps as we seek to internalize and live from God's truth.

Step 1: Begin to Notice Your Thoughts

God wants us to be honest with Him—and ourselves—about what is going on in our heads. He cares deeply about this because our thoughts have a direct impact on all aspects of our lives, including our parenting. Our thoughts give us a window into our hearts, helping us understand the parts of ourselves that we need to change with God's loving help.

For too many years, I knew that God was all-knowing, but this had a relatively small impact on my life. I didn't think like someone who knew his thoughts were on full display before the sovereign Creator and sustainer of the universe. This didn't change until I entered my early forties and began to experience the gospel on a much deeper level, becoming awestruck by the price paid by Christ to free me from my sin. The immensity of His love—His willingness to suffer and die for me—opened my eyes. It gradually became clear that my negative thinking, in which I dwelled on my failures and beat myself up over them, was not consistent with His truth. He also showed me that this mental habit was wearing me out, making it hard for me to practice the patient, loving, and strong parenting that I preached to others.

Since that time, I have seen that I am not the only one who struggles with this problem. Many Christians miss out on the peace and strength God wants them to enjoy because they believe their thoughts don't matter if they can keep them a secret. Shame and secrecy are the key factors that keep many people enslaved to habits they want to break. They try to hide their thoughts from God, attempting to solve these problems without His help.

Satan loves it when this happens. He gains power over us only when we try to go it alone, knowing it won't be long before we're exhausted and feeling defeated. Pouncing on us in this weakened state, he feeds these feelings with false accusations that overwhelm our thinking:

If you were a good parent, you'd never get short with your kids or raise your voice at them.

If you were a good parent, your kids would be more compliant and appreciative for what they have.

If you were a good parent, your kids would be showing a lot more spiritual growth.
If you just work harder to get your act together, God will bless you with better-behaved kids.
It's too late. You've already made so many mistakes with your kids that there is no hope.

Discouraging lies like these lead to great pain, which results in less joy and effectiveness with our kids. Regardless of what might be keeping you from growing as a parent, whether it be difficulty being assertive with your kids, rescuing them too often, losing your temper, having perfectionistic tendencies, feeling defeated, or any other struggle, the path to healing starts with confessing to God what He already knows. Lay your thoughts before Him, confident that He won't gasp in shock, chastise, or abandon you. Remember that He is "the God of compassion and mercy . . . slow to anger and filled with unfailing love and faithfulness" (Exodus 34:6, NLT). Likewise, remember: "If we confess our sins to him, he is faithful and just to forgive us our sins and to cleanse us from all wickedness" (1 John 1:9, NLT). Yes, the truth will set you free.

Step 2: Adopt a Level and Plumb Line for Your Thinking

As a teen, I worked summers on a construction crew. One of my most memorable assignments was helping my boss, Jon, build a brick home. I quickly learned that seemingly insignificant errors quickly added up to a wall so crooked that it was useless. To build a straight and strong wall, this wise man showed me how to check each brick against a level and a plumb line (a heavy brass weight hanging on a string). Using the level allowed me to continually correct errors with the horizontal placement of bricks. The plumb line allowed me to fix any vertical lean gradually developing in the wall. As I worked, it gave me great comfort to know that I could make corrections before it was too late.

Jon was not only a skilled craftsman but he was also gifted at equating everything we did to deeper life principles. "Every time we believe something that is even just a slight bit wrong, our lives begin to tilt," he cautioned. "We can't serve God if our heads aren't on straight and our thinking isn't on the level."

Biblical principles serve as our spiritual level and plumb line. They prevent us from falling for the lies that this world and the devil would love for us to believe. For instance, note how Scripture corrects two common parenting misperceptions. The first incorrectly equates love with leniency:

> **Lie:** If *you discipline your children, it will stunt their emotional growth and creativity.*
> **Truth:** *Loving discipline prevents children from facing a life of pain.*

> Discipline your children while there is hope.
> Otherwise you will ruin their lives.
> **PROVERBS 19:18, NLT**

The second false belief centers on a misunderstanding of how we should reflect God's strength to our kids:

> **Lie:** *When your kids misbehave, they need to see how angry it makes you.*
> **Truth:** *Fully expressing anger and frustration as we discipline does not model the self-discipline we want them to develop.*

> A fool gives full vent to his spirit,
> but a wise man quietly holds it back.
> **PROVERBS 29:11**

Obviously, to keep our thoughts aligned with God's Word, we must consistently read and understand the Bible. While true, this thought can be overwhelming. If you struggle to comprehend what you read in the Bible, please don't panic! You don't have to perfectly understand every part of it. The only thing you need is a heart that deeply desires to follow God. This pleases Him deeply, and He will take your hand and show you the way.

As a young person, I was imprisoned by such fear, failing to take joy in a simple sense of curiosity about what God has to say about Himself and His creation. A dear friend of mine gave me some advice that changed my life. He said something like this:

> Charles, stop seeing it as a "have to" and begin enjoying it as a "want to." If you start by spending just a tiny bit of time with the Bible each day, reading and wondering what God is trying to tell you, you will begin to get more curious about it every day. The more curious you get, the more you will find yourself hungering for understanding. The hungrier you get, the more you will seek out the truth by discussing your questions with godly people, studying good articles and books, listening to sermons, and doing whatever you can to solve the mysteries about the Bible in your mind. You might just find yourself being dissatisfied with spending only a small amount of time with it.

God desires that we come to Him out of free will and love, not out of cold obligation. When we are motivated by love, He will multiply our love for His Word and our joy in studying it.

Aligning Your Thoughts with God's Truth

Drawing on God's strength requires frequent prayer in which we admit our feelings, acknowledge what we are thinking, ask God to share His truth, and seek His help in aligning our thoughts and feelings with His. As you identify and then seek to address the wrong beliefs in your life, you may find the following practice helpful.

MY PRAYER FOR TRUTH

- Dear Lord, I have been feeling

  ____

- I have found myself thinking:

  ____

  ____

- Lord, what does Your Word teach about this?

  ____

  ____

- Lord, please help me dwell on what You say is true and on nothing else. I want my deepest thoughts and beliefs to reflect Your goodness.

Below are some examples from my work with parents:

Example: A parent with young children

† Dear Lord, I have been feeling *stressed and exhausted in my role as a parent. I feel like the kids never listen to a thing I say.*

† I have found myself thinking: *I don't measure up. I don't have what it takes. I shouldn't be having so much trouble with this.*

† Lord, what does Your Word teach about this? *I must put my faith in Your strength and not my own abilities. You say that Your power is made perfect in weakness. You love me and are pleased when I ask You for help.*

- † Lord, please help me dwell on what You say is true and on nothing else. I want my deepest thoughts and beliefs to reflect Your goodness.

Example: A parent struggling with being permissive

- † Dear Lord, I have been feeling *worried about my relationship with my teenage son. I've also been concerned that he is getting out of control.*
- † I have found myself thinking: *If I discipline him, he will get mad and our relationship will be ruined.*
- † Lord, what does Your Word teach about this? *Worrying doesn't accomplish anything positive. We must discipline our children. Discipline is an act of love.*
- † Lord, please help me dwell on what You say is true and on nothing else. I want my deepest thoughts and beliefs to reflect Your goodness.

Example: A parent dealing with anger toward their child

- † Dear Lord, I have been feeling *very angry toward my child. I feel guilty for feeling that way, but then I go right back to being mad at them when they do something wrong.*
- † I have found myself thinking: *I'm a bad parent for feeling so angry at my child. They are blessings from God. I don't know why I feel this way so much.*
- † Lord, what does Your Word teach about this? *Children are a blessing from You. It's okay for me to feel anger if I don't say or do something hurtful* and *I don't hold on to anger for long periods of time. Praying for others we are angry with is very important. My children need my prayer. I need prayer. I need to let other people help me with the kids and all of the other things I have on my plate.*
- † Lord, please help me dwell on what You say is true and on nothing else. I want my deepest thoughts and beliefs to reflect Your goodness.

Step 3: Ask God to Help You Evaluate and Change the Deeper Beliefs Behind Your Faulty Thinking

The third step involves developing a strong curiosity about how your thinking compares to God's level and plumb line. It requires you to go deeper and consider whether your actions and attitudes truly line up with what you say you believe. Asking Him to guide you as you read Scripture will help you see and evaluate both your stated, or formal, beliefs and your deeper functional beliefs.

What do I mean by formal and functional beliefs? Icebergs are a great way of explaining them. Each iceberg has two parts: the beautiful portion floating above the water's surface and the much bigger, potentially dangerous part submerged below.

Like the visible part of the iceberg, your formal beliefs float above the surface, clearly observable to everyone, including yourself. They are the pretty part, as they represent ideas consistent with what you think "good Christian people" should believe.

Functional beliefs, on the other hand, represent the largest yet often unseen part of your mind, and they have the greatest impact on how you function. These beliefs are extremely powerful, impacting your actions most when you know no one is watching or when you are tempted by strong emotions. The *Titanic* sank when it struck the iceberg's hidden part. It's a great reminder that what is hidden—including the beliefs you act on—can destroy your life.

The distinction between formal and functional beliefs helps explain why a mom may teach her daughter to be patient with and forgive others yet gives her daughter the silent treatment after she has made just one mistake. If this mom is spiritually curious, she wonders about this disconnect and is eager to have light shed upon the deepest parts of her mind and heart. Because of this, she asks God and godly people to help her explore these depths. She wants to follow Christ's command to be patient and forgiving, but she realizes that when she freezes out her daughter, she is reenacting her parents' response to her own misbehavior as a girl. She grows in spiritual maturity as there is increasing agreement between her formal beliefs and the functional ones she often lives by.

We can confidently ask God to help us as we seek to align our beliefs with His, knowing that abiding in Christ is the only path to freedom: "Jesus said to the Jews who had believed him, 'If you abide in my word, you are truly my disciples, and you will know the truth, and the truth will set you free'" (John 8:31-32).

I feel compelled to provide a warning as you begin to work through these steps and become aware of any false beliefs you've been holding: If you rely on *self-control* to confront and do battle with inaccurate or self-defeating thoughts, it will only and always result in feelings of shame and failure.

If you rely on *self-control* to confront and do battle with inaccurate or self-defeating thoughts, it will only and always result in feelings of shame and failure.

Focusing on any unwanted habit with the intent of eliminating it through personal effort actually increases its power. When we rely on our own willpower, the root causes of sin and despair go unaddressed, and the underlying problem either remains or resurfaces in a different form. This is the whack-a-mole approach to self-improvement. Yes, we are called to devote effort to our growth, but such effort is effective only when it is empowered by God. As the Good Physician, He is the only one capable of curing our spiritual maladies.

PASSING ON TRUTH TO YOUR KIDS

Perhaps the biggest benefit in allowing God to change the way you think is the greater strength, patience, and grace this will help you demonstrate as you guide your kids toward Him and His ways. The more your thinking and actions coincide with His truth, the more consistently your parenting style will bring glory to Him—and be really good for them! In the next chapter, you will see how this style also affects the emotional, moral, and spiritual growth of your children, even in ways that you might not realize.

Ultimately, you cannot *make* your kids love God. You can, however, parent in ways that help them learn about His commandments, discover His loving grace, and act in godly ways.

CHAPTER 3

A HEALTHY PARENTING STYLE FOR A STRONG RELATIONSHIP

Teaching Love and Respect

Every Sunday morning the same story of chaos and confusion unfolded in Joel and Abby's home. With four children—ages thirteen, six, two, and four months—the couple found the task of getting everyone out the door and to church on time a major undertaking. Someone was always sleeping past the alarm; someone was always fighting for more time in the bathroom; someone was always dawdling with toys rather than getting dressed. Abby had to get ready in spurts because she was constantly interrupted by requests for more breakfast or to referee a sibling conflict. Often she had to raise her voice a few times before the kids knew she was serious and followed her direction.

One particularly disastrous morning, Abby sighed loudly as she marched back to her room for what felt like the hundredth time after resolving a sibling squabble. As she passed Joel putting on his shoes, she made a snappy comment: "Why do I always have to do all the work and keep the kids in line?"

Joel was irritated. Why couldn't they have a peaceful Sunday morning? Abby and the kids seemed to constantly be complaining, whining, and creating drama. That's why, walking into the kitchen, Joel was amazed to find that their six-year-old, Becky, was dressed and ready before anyone else. "Daddy, can you help me with this puzzle?" she asked.

Joel, always wanting to show his love for his kids, sat with her and quickly lost track of time. Suddenly, he was reminded of more pressing matters as Abby called, "Joel, can you give me a little help here?"

Joel sighed, torn. "Sorry, honey," he said to Becky. "How about we finish this afternoon?" He hated the look of disappointment on her face, but after giving her a quick hug, Joel left the room.

In response to Abby's obvious frustration, Joel rushed around the house, helping the kids find misplaced sweaters, coats, shoes, and Bibles. At the last minute, he also revved up the vacuum and a duster, trying to rescue the kids from the consequences of scattering most of their breakfast on the kitchen floor.

By the time Joel and Abby managed to get the kids in the car, the tension was at an all-time high. They said nothing to each other, though when a few of the kids began squabbling, Abby turned around and said, "Enough!" The car was silent for the rest of the trip—and, of course, they were late again.

As they pulled into the parking lot, Joel whipped into the one open spot a zip code away from the building. Madison, their thirteen-year-old, rolled her eyes and complained, "Why do we even go to church when we just fight when we do? It's not like we really do any of the stuff Pastor Rob talks about."

They rushed into the building, listening to the worship team lead the congregation in "It Is Well with My Soul." The disconnect between this hymn and how Joel and Abby felt made their hearts ache.

When Joel and Abby were first married, they loved to imagine what their family rhythms would look like, how they would treat each other with love and respect. That seemed impossible now. They first came to see me because they knew they needed a better plan, not just for Sunday mornings, but for their parenting overall.

IS YOUR PARENTING STYLE TEACHING LOVE AND RESPECT?

I wonder if you've ever had a Sunday morning like Joel and Abby's. I know I have! Remember, God's grace shines most brilliantly on our worst days, in our times of greatest need. Parenthood has countless benefits. One of the least recognized yet most important is how it can help us recognize our need for Christ. When we reach the end of our abilities and strength, we most vividly experience His strength and love: "My grace is all you need. My power works best in weakness" (2 Corinthians 12:9, NLT).

When we consider the role God has given us in teaching our children—especially in these difficult moments—it can be helpful to pause and begin by taking an honest look at ourselves and how our actions are contributing to the difficulty we are experiencing. Is our dominant parenting style giving our kids the best opportunity to learn how to love and respect God and other people? Is it contributing to peace in our home, or might it be contributing to conflict? In the early 1980s my father, Jim Fay, and his colleague Foster W. Cline, MD, observed three distinct parenting styles—helicopter, drill sergeant, and consultant.[1]

What Is Your Parenting Style?

Are you raising kids who are mentally strong or weak? Your parenting style plays a key role. Helicopter and drill sergeant (along with permissive) parenting styles often contribute to a lack of motivation, neediness, anxiety, a lack of self-control, feelings of entitlement, and other problems. The consultant style facilitates the development of confidence, respect, resilience, and self-control. What's your primary style?*

1. Do you routinely feel like you take more responsibility for your child's schoolwork than they do?
2. Do you often give your kid—regardless of their age—detailed instructions for doing things that they already know how to do or could figure out on their own?
3. Are you mostly hands-off when it comes to your child?
4. Do you work hard to purposely guide your child to own and solve their own problems?
5. Do you too frequently try to solve problems for your child because it makes you feel good inside?
6. When your child makes a mistake, do you get angry, scold, then feel guilty about it and rescue them?
7. Does your fear of upsetting your kid often keep you from setting and enforcing limits they really need?
8. Do you guide your child to learn by asking, "What do you think you might do about this?" when they come to you with a problem?
9. Do you too often try to protect your child from life's stresses and obstacles?
10. Do you find yourself making threats that you don't follow through on?
11. Do you give your kid free rein to do whatever they want without much supervision?
12. Do you allow your child to make affordable mistakes and experience the consequences, even though you would rather rescue them?

* Note: This parenting style quiz is intended to provide general information only; it isn't intended to diagnose, treat, or prevent any condition. Always consult a mental health professional if you have a mental health concern.

13. Do you often feel stressed because you are constantly planning for your child's days and worrying about entertaining them?
14. Do you stonewall (not talk to), ignore, belittle, shame, or react with sarcasm when angry with your child?
15. Do you ignore difficult behavior, hoping it will just go away?
16. When you set limits and rules, do you consistently enforce them with empathy and coaching?

Answering yes to questions 1, 5, 9, and 13 indicates a helicopter approach to parenting.

Answering yes to questions 2, 6, 10, and 14 reflects a drill sergeant approach.

Answering yes to questions 4, 8, 12, and 16 indicates a consultant approach.

Another common approach is permissive parenting. Answering yes to questions 3, 7, 11, and 15 reflects this style.

The Helicopter Style

Helicopters are in the business of search and rescue. Parents who adopt this style too often hover over their children unnecessarily, attempting to control their lives by rescuing them from even the smallest trials. They work overtime to ensure that their children do not experience any consequences because of their poor decisions. They also stunt their children's emotional and spiritual growth by protecting them from trials that God can use to build maturity. To be sure, rescuing our children from very serious consequences is the right thing to do. It's very damaging, however, when we make a habit of needlessly rescuing them from consequences and challenges they can learn from.

Joel began to see that he was spending way too much time doing things for the kids that they could learn to do for themselves. By doing so, he was shielding them from making any real decisions and having to live with the consequences. Though well-intentioned, this parenting approach left Joel exhausted, hurt his relationship with his wife, and sent a damaging underlying message to his kids. Instead of expressing true love and respect, it told them: "You are not capable. If you were, I wouldn't have to do everything for you."

Joel learned that his helicopter habits were motivated and maintained by anxiety. He was attempting to make every situation his kids faced neat and clean. He was always trying to keep them happy. "I began to realize that God often uses the messiness of life—and the suffering that sometimes comes along with it—to shape our kids' character," he told me. "By trying to rescue them all the time, I was fighting against Him."

At this point, it's important to emphasize what God's Word tells us about hardships. As loving parents, they are the last thing we *want* our kids to experience. Could it be, however, that our kids *must* face them to grow spiritually strong? God tells us through the apostle Paul,

> We can rejoice, too, when we run into problems and trials, for we know that they help us develop endurance. And endurance develops strength of character, and character strengthens our confident hope of salvation. And this hope will not lead to disappointment. For we know how dearly God loves us, because he has given us the Holy Spirit to fill our hearts with his love.
>
> **ROMANS 5:3-5, NLT**

Please don't beat yourself up if you discover that you have some helicopter-like habits. I struggle with them. Many people do. In 2023, the Amen Clinics created a parenting style quiz that participants could take online. Fifty-two percent of the 3,522 people who completed it provided responses indicating that their dominant style was to helicopter. With God's help, you can change, and your children can thrive. Remember that you are still God's masterpiece as you pray this simple prayer:

Please, Lord, help me recognize when it's best for me to step back, take a deep breath, and allow my kids to do more things for themselves. Please help me remember that the small consequences and trials they face now will help them avoid having to face much larger ones later.

The Drill Sergeant Style

As opposed to the helicopter parent, a drill sergeant parent too often issues orders, attempting to ensure that their children avoid even the smallest mistakes. Although it's wise for us to step in and do our best to stop our kids from making extremely costly mistakes, people who overuse the drill sergeant style try to stop their children from making *any* mistakes. By doing so, they deprive them of affordable learning opportunities and end up fighting many control battles.

God allows us to make mistakes and to experience the consequences. This is one of the many ways He helps us learn how much we need Him and how important it is to serve Him. When Jesus was being falsely accused and was soon to be executed, Peter, one of His closest disciples, worried that he might suffer the same fate. Out of fear, Peter denied that he knew Jesus three separate times. As a result, Peter suffered great anguish. Jesus, being God, was certainly capable of keeping this from happening. Instead, He allowed it, restored Peter, and recommissioned him to be a great leader of the church. Jesus also used this to show all readers of the Bible, throughout all history, the magnitude of His grace, the importance of serving Him, and the fact that obedience may lead to persecution (see John 18:15-27; 21:15-19).

Abby realized something: She had forgotten that we all benefit from the freedom to learn through our mistakes. As a result, she had fallen into the habit of constantly nagging, reminding, and lecturing the kids. Her attempts to stay on top of everything and everyone left her with little time and energy left to take care of her own needs and her responsibility to be a supportive wife and mother.

As she thought through a typical Sunday morning, Abby began to see that her attempts to micromanage her kids were robbing them of low-cost learning opportunities, hurting her relationship with Joel, resulting in unneeded conflict with the kids, and leaving her constantly worn out. She realized that the message she sent by acting like a drill sergeant also limited her ability to teach love and respect. Instead, the unstated message she was sending her family was: "You are not capable. If you were, I wouldn't always have to tell you what to do."

If you overuse the drill sergeant style, you aren't alone either. Twenty percent of the parents completing the parenting survey provided responses indicating that this was their dominant style. From time to time, I've also fallen into the trap of micromanaging and trying to direct my kids by raising the decibel of my voice.

Our parenting challenges, many of which are rooted in our struggles with ourselves, are no surprise to God. Remember, He knew you before the beginning of time, and He loves you and your kids beyond comprehension. Nothing can separate you from the love of God. As you seek to find a better way to teach your kids how to love and respect others, you might pray this prayer:

Please, Lord, help me recognize when I am feeling tempted to control my kids by telling them what to do or by yelling. Comfort me with the reminder that they will come to love and respect me more if I allow them to learn from making plenty of affordable mistakes.

These first two styles create children who tend to have a harder time making good decisions, behaving responsibly, and treating others in loving and respectful ways. These also lead to more power struggles, parent-child conflict, and disagreements over parenting. The third style, which we'll look at next, represents the ideal in most situations, since it builds stronger and more peaceful relationships by modeling love and respect.

The Consultant Style

At Love and Logic, we call the healthier style consultant parenting. As the name implies, consultant parents teach by modeling loving and respectful behavior, providing solid information, and allowing their children to make plenty of decisions. But don't be fooled—these parents are not permissive or hands-off. As you will see throughout the remainder of this book, they set firm limits and hold their children accountable for the consequences of their actions. They allow their children to learn from the natural consequences of their actions. It's also important to note that these parents give themselves permission to occasionally act a bit like helicopters or drill sergeants when their kids are in imminent danger.

After learning about these three styles, Abby had an important realization: "I started thinking about how God parents us. He isn't anxious about us messing up. Even though He is the King of kings, He doesn't micromanage everything we do. He doesn't get bent out of shape when we have to learn lessons the hard way. He lets us goof and gives us the grace we need to grow. I'd like to be more like that with the kids and Joel." With love and respect, consultant parents exercise full authority, never hesitating to say no when they need to. They intentionally allow their children to make plenty of decisions over small matters, all the while doing their best to avoid rescuing or micromanaging. As a result, they teach their kids to make responsible decisions in bigger matters and send a message conducive to teaching love and respect: "Every choice you make has consequences. You are capable of learning from the ones you make."

This approach, and the strong relationship it builds with our children, shows them what it looks like to be motivated by the desire to love and respect God and our neighbors. We can help them develop this attitude from the heart, rather than simply learning to fake it to manipulate others. Seeking this goal, pray the following:

Dear Lord Jesus, please give me the wisdom and strength to let my children make the decisions they need to make, to allow them to face the consequences they need to experience, and to guide them with the strength and love You have shown me.

WHY BUILDING RELATIONSHIPS AND TRUST MATTERS SO MUCH

When learning about these parenting styles, some parents become overwhelmed with shame and fear. It's not my desire to leave you feeling this way. My goal is to remind you that God is graceful and that His truth will set you free to discover more effective and joy-filled ways to parent. When Joel reflected on his upbringing, he recognized his own parents' dominant style. He told me, "My parents always insisted on good behavior, but I never felt very connected with them. I think that's why I did a lot of things behind their back that I knew were wrong. It was my way of rebelling. I think I would have felt a lot more remorse for acting this way if we'd had a close relationship."

Joel hit on something important: We cannot truly love and respect anyone until we feel safe in our relationship with them. This is why effective parents also take time to look into their children's eyes, provide loving touch, smile at them, and consistently meet their needs. Building trust in this way helps us raise virtuous and spiritually strong kids. Why is this? When young people are emotionally bonded with their parents, they are far more likely to adopt their parents' core values. They are also more likely to make healthy choices even when they are away from home. They are more likely to learn to obey out of love and respect rather than fear.

We cannot truly love and respect anyone until we feel safe in our relationship with them.

The Trust Cycle: Parents and Child

It is never too early to begin this attachment and bonding process. In fact, it's essential that we start as soon as our kids are born. During babies' first year of life outside the womb, a wonderful sequence begins and repeats itself, giving them intimate experience with our trustworthiness. Because we represent God to them at this time, they have an opportunity to learn about His trustworthiness and provision through the following cycle:

Infants experience intense needs that, if unmet, threaten their survival. They may discover they're hungry. They may be cold. They may feel lonely. They may need their diaper changed. Regardless of the specific problem, they are in a near constant state of need. If these are not met, they will not survive physically or emotionally.

They cry for help. Once outside the womb an infant has their first experience seeking help. "Please save me!" is their cry translated into words.

We meet their needs. Empowered by the love of God, we identify each need and meet it. In the process we communicate His delight in them by smiling, looking into their eyes, providing the warmth of touch, and communicating loving care through our voices.

One parent told me, "It blew me away when I really came to grips with the fact that I represent God to my little baby. She looks to me for everything she needs. It makes me even more thankful that He is giving me the strength to do this."

Trust develops. Because we come when they call, the seeds of trust begin to grow. With this trust comes the capacity to sincerely love and respect others. This is what it means to have a conscience. Doesn't it make sense that our children will find it easier to trust God when they are secure in their ability to trust us?

The cycle repeats. Anyone who has cared for an infant knows that they have multiple needs each and every twenty-four-hour period!

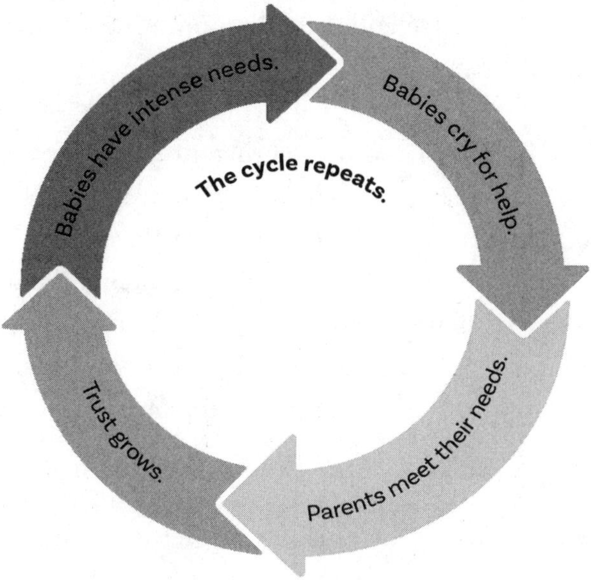

The Trust Cycle: God and Our Children

The cycle just described represents how a trust relationship develops between parent and child. A very similar pattern can strengthen our children's trust in God later on as they encounter the inevitable trials of life:

God acts and provides. The Lord is always active and providing for our kids, even when we are tempted to believe He isn't. The truest form of spiritual strength is faith that He is working all things for our good even when it seems like He isn't. It is this faith that comforts us and our children with a joy that defies our circumstances and expands our comprehension of His trustworthiness.

Our children have plenty of opportunities to see that God provides comfort even when He doesn't change our situation. They will also learn a great deal about this by watching us as we reflect confidence and strength while enduring disappointing or downright difficult circumstances.

Our children face events and circumstances that test their faith. They will encounter many trials during their lifetimes. These will likely include financial challenges, illnesses, deaths of loved ones, painful relationship betrayals, parenting challenges, natural disasters, and other difficult events or circumstances. The more they experience God when they are young, the more likely they will become young adults who respond with faith rather than overwhelming fear.

They cry out to God. Our heavenly Father is delighted when His children come to Him in humble desperation: "Please, Father, I need Your help!" We can pray that our children develop this habit as early in their lives as possible.

Spiritual strength grows. Each time our kids witness God's provision in the midst of pain, turmoil, and fear, their spiritual strength expands.

The cycle repeats. As long as we and our kids live in earthly bodies, there will be no end to events and circumstances that test our faith. Fortunately, God will never abandon us.

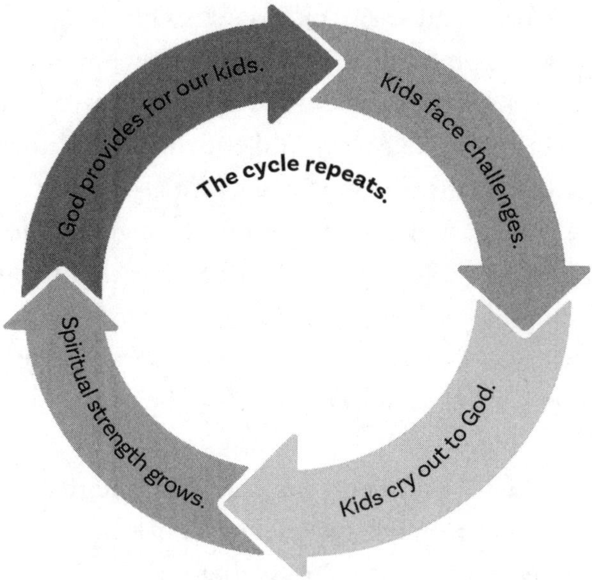

Some people question, *What do trust, faith, and spiritual strength have to do with raising loving and respectful kids?* The answer is obvious when we consider what happens when faith and trust are absent: fear. Like oil and water, fear cannot occupy the same space as love or respect. This is why the least loving and respectful people are the most consumed with fear, and the most loving and respectful are filled with faith and trust.

Through constant repetition, we pass on the lessons of dependency, trust, faith, respect, and love to our kids. In the process, we reinforce truths about God:

- He is present and sees them.
- He delights in them and is absolutely crazy about spending time with them.
- He hears their cries.
- He knows what they need, and He meets those needs.

If you look back and wish you'd done some things differently as a parent, please remember that God is infinitely more powerful than your mistakes and any situations you've faced. And even if your parents didn't engage in this cycle of love and trust with you, there is always hope because God is the true source of spiritual strength. There is also hope because these cycles of trust continue throughout our lives, offering us endless opportunities to learn trust and teach it to our children.

If you're hoping to provide an even stronger foundation of love and respect for your kids, these ten essential questions can be a way to consider where you might improve:

1. At least twice a day, do I take the initiative to connect with my children through eye contact, smiles, and loving touch?
2. Do I make it clear that I miss them when we are apart?
3. Do I sit with them for at least one meal every day?
4. Do I pray with and for them?
5. Do I empathize and listen when they are upset and celebrate with them when they are happy?
6. Every day, do I set aside at least a few minutes of downtime so that we can be together without distractions?
7. Do I spend more time helping them discover their God-given strengths than pointing out what they do wrong?
8. Do I allow them to make mistakes and demonstrate that I love them even when they do?
9. Do I show them love and respect by allowing them to experience trials and then see that they are capable of coping with them?
10. Do I spend far more time interacting with them than interacting with my devices?

Dear reader, I confess that my own answers to these questions aren't always yes. It's important that you know that I have struggled with everything I am writing about. Please don't be overwhelmed or discouraged by these questions. Use them as an opportunity for growth and a reminder of your desperate need for grace, never forgetting that "there is therefore now no condemnation for those who are in Christ Jesus" (Romans 8:1). God desires the very best for you and your kids, and He knows the warfare that is being waged against you and your children. Jesus understands our frailties and our daily struggles to become the godly parents we want to be—and He stands ready to help:

> For we do not have a high priest who is unable to sympathize with our weaknesses, but one who in every respect has been tempted as we are, yet without sin. Let us then with confidence draw near to the throne of grace, that we may receive mercy and find grace to help in time of need.
>
> HEBREWS 4:15-16

A PATH FORWARD

As Joel and Abby practiced parenting from a consultant perspective and gradually abandoned their helicopter and drill sergeant ways, they were excited to see their home begin to grow calmer. With honest reflection, they realized that their "Sunday morning problem" was not really a problem. It was a *symptom* signaling an opportunity to reconnect and to seek authentic relationships and joy with their kids.

Their hearts were changing, but they needed some specific action steps to help them keep from falling back into the rut they'd slipped into. I recommended several steps to get them started in strengthening their relationships with their kids, and I offer them to you as well:

1. **Get focused on your real and most important motivation for connecting with your kids.** For most parents, there are two things that motivate their desire to build strong

relationships with their kids. The first is their unconditional love for them. The second is their hope that their kids will become more cooperative and well-behaved. Both of these motivations are good ones, but the first should be the primary driving force.

Have you ever known someone who related to you in a primarily transactional manner, where it was clear that they were acting friendly, kind, or cooperative because they wanted something in return? I hope you also know someone who is kind and loving toward you, expecting nothing in return. Which of these relationships is the healthiest and most fulfilling? Which is real?

Martin and his wife, Anastasia, decided to implement a variety of Love and Logic techniques to improve their relationship with their twelve-year-old daughter, Alexis, hoping that this would tone down her defiance. Sensing change in her mom and dad, Alexis became suspicious, feeling as if they were trying to manipulate her into behaving. As a result, she tested their intentions by being even more argumentative.

Fortunately, Martin and Anastasia's main motivation was their deep and unconditional love for their daughter. Instead of applying a "system," they were showing her what was already in their hearts. This is fortunate, because consider what might have happened if their primary motivation had been to create a more compliant child. They would have become discouraged, may have felt resentful, and certainly would have gone back to their old and less-than-optimal parenting. Systems are temporary. Relationships are everlasting.

Because they didn't let their daughter's grumbling deter them from showing their loving-kindness, she eventually began to trust that their actions were sincere. With this realization, she did become more cooperative and well-behaved.

This happened because Martin and Anastasia did not try to use their relationship with her as a tool. Their affection was simply what naturally flowed from their hearts when they were no longer burdened by the stress of trying to parent as helicopters or drill sergeants. Anastasia put it well, "When we stopped trying to control her and allowed her to face the natural consequences of her actions, we felt freer to love her."

2. **For each of your kids, make a list of at least six things they like or like to do.** Healthy relationships are built by observing what our kids value. Noticing the little things communicates that we cherish our kids so much that we even care about the smallest details. In this way, we emulate our heavenly Father, who even knows the number of hairs on our head (see Luke 12:7). One of the many wonderful names for God in the Hebrew Bible is *El Roi*, "The God who sees me."

> Noticing the little things our kids value communicates that we cherish them so much that we even care about the smallest details.

A good way to begin this practice is to write out some statements about what you notice, using the following format: "I noticed that you ________________." Some examples:

"I noticed that you like to draw horses."
"I noticed that you are really getting into baseball."
"I noticed that you like to play with this doll."
"I noticed that you run fast in those shoes."
"I noticed that you really seem happy about your car."
"I noticed that your friends look up to you."
"I noticed that you can skip."
"I noticed that you really like to pet our dog."

"I noticed that you really like to learn about planets and solar systems."
"I noticed that you are growing."
"I noticed that you like to look at that."
"I noticed that you prefer reading adventure stories."
"I noticed that you really like to laugh."
"I noticed that you like to make others laugh."

As you can see from these examples, noticing just about any positive quality, interest, or skill qualifies. It's also important to remember that it is the *act of noticing* that makes the difference, not so much *what* we notice.

3. **Approach each of your kids at least twice a week and share something you have noticed.** Do this only when you are alone with them and doing so won't embarrass them.

   As you share your "I noticed" statements, hug them, place your hand lovingly on their shoulder, give them a fist bump, high five, or some other form of touch. Smile and glance into their eyes.

   Listen if they want to talk, but don't force the issue. If they seem uncomfortable, give them some space. Some children and teens are likely to respond by rolling their eyes and saying something like "You are so weird, Dad!" or "What do you want, Mom?" Don't take this personally. Just smile and say something like "I know" or "I just noticed that you like that."

4. **Avoid ending your "I noticed" statements above with "That's great!" or some other form of praise.** Praise is not always harmful, but it can be. Too frequently it is perceived as a form of evaluation or judgment. Children who struggle

with insecurity often think, *If this person thinks that this is great, they will also think that something else about me isn't.*

Children raised with excessive praise may learn to place a high premium on pleasing others. Once developed, this people-pleasing habit can become a significant hindrance to healthy emotional and spiritual growth.

Many parents wonder, *Is it ever okay to praise my kids?* Spontaneous, authentic praise is wonderful. Praise that is forced or is used with the intention to build self-concept or reward good behavior is much riskier. A far safer strategy is to notice what they have done by saying something like "You held the door open for those people. I noticed that." As strange as it may seem, this is often far more reinforcing to our kids than us going over the top with enthusiasm. This is even truer with children who have a hard time hearing praise.

For some still unknown reason, one of my sons almost consistently reacted poorly to praise. He would either argue that the good things I was commenting on were not so good, put himself down, or act out a bit to prove that I was wrong to think he could do anything good. I will never forget the day he hit a home run. I had been learning a lot about how to respond to kids like him, so I experimented with curbing my enthusiasm and just said, "I noticed that you hit that ball hard." Then I shut my mouth. This was one of the hardest things I've ever done, but it was also one of the most effective. He smiled from ear to ear and cheerfully replied, "Yeah, I smashed it over the wall!"

Joel and Abby, like countless other parents, discovered a number of positive things after just two weeks of intentionally noticing what their kids loved or were good at. Abby told me, "Doing this helped me get focused on what is most important, and my attitude started to change. I always knew that I loved the kids, but I started to realize that I really like them too! Madison has been the biggest challenge for me, possibly because she is so much like me. Using the ideas you shared with me, I started putting two rubber bands around my left wrist every morning. I put them there to remind me to stop twice every day and notice little things that might make her feel good. Each day, I noticed things like the fact that she likes to play her guitar, she is getting taller, she loves her grandma, she is becoming more independent, or she has a lot of interesting ideas about politics. One day I was a bit lost about what to notice, so I ended up saying, 'I noticed that you enjoy using your debating skills.'"

As I heard this, I laughed and asked Abby, "You really said that?"

She replied, "Oh, yes. I said it nicely with no sarcasm, but I kind of surprised myself."

"How did she react?" I inquired.

"She replied in a very calm and matter-of-fact way," Abby answered. "She said, 'I know what you guys are doing. It's that stuff you are learning at those meetings with that doctor.'"

"She's a bright kid!" I said. "How did you respond?"

"All I could think to do was hug her and say, 'Well, is it working?' She hugged me back and said jokingly, 'I noticed that you and Dad are making a really good effort.'"

Joel also agreed that the approach was helping. "Yes, at first our older kids were pretty suspicious. Now they are talking with us a lot more about what excites them, and we are having a lot of fun conversations."

"The biggest takeaway for me," said Joel, "is that I know for sure I'm more relaxed and able to have a lot more fun with all of them. This has really helped with Madison, who has aways reacted very poorly when either Abby or I start getting uptight. The other day she told me she loved me. It's been a long time since I heard that."

"How about little Becky?" I asked. "How is she reacting?"

Joel smiled. "She loves it. I noticed that she liked butterflies. Now she's asked me to read the same book about monarchs what seems like a thousand times. It's been a lot of fun for both of us."

Focusing on parenting styles and deliberately building trust, however, doesn't resolve *every* family issue; we also need to set effective limits to help our children develop humility and obedience. In the next chapter, we'll see how Joel and Abby began implementing limits as they sought to tame the Sunday morning chaos in their home. As they discovered, helping children develop a strong faith and character requires both building a loving relationship *and* helping them learn how to submit to loving authority. Essentially, they wanted to model for their kids the way Christ calls us to honor His authority:

> If you love me, you will keep my commandments. And I will ask the Father, and he will give you another Helper, to be with you forever, even the Spirit of truth, whom the world cannot receive, because it neither sees him nor knows him. You know him, for he dwells with you and will be in you.
>
> **JOHN 14:15-17**

When children learn to live within loving limits, they begin to experience how faith starts as a gift of God yet grows through action: We love Christ because He first loved us. We obey Him because we love Him. Our love for Him grows as we obey Him.

CHAPTER 4

LOVING LIMITS

Developing Humility and Obedience

Pushing the grocery cart toward the checkout line, Emily silently prayed, *Please, Lord, give me the strength to get through this shopping trip without losing my temper.*

The trip had been exhausting. Two-year-old Samantha had been a handful. Getting her into her car seat required advanced gymnastic skills, and Emily wondered if her own hearing had been permanently damaged by the volume of the tantrum that lasted for the entire twenty-minute drive to the store. Once she parked, the trial continued. The seat Sam once hated was now her favorite spot. Instead of simply getting out and cooperating as Emily tried to move her into the shopping cart, Sam fought her mother every step of the way. Emily held it together, but just barely.

The checkout line was like Los Angeles's I-5 at rush hour. Their progress slowed even more once the harried clerk spoke into his microphone, "Price check. I need a price check." Of course, they were stalled in a spot decorated with endless impulse-buy temptations. Hanging just within Sam's reach was forbidden fruit—a candy bar. A smile formed on her beautiful little face, her eyes brightened, and she snagged it from the rack.

It was a small, ordinary moment, but Emily was faced with a big decision: How was she going to respond? Would she raise her voice and threaten Sam if she didn't put the candy back, give in and buy her the candy bar, or calmly set and enforce a limit?

WHY LIMITS ARE LIFE-GIVING

In the previous chapter I emphasized that infants are completely unable to meet their own needs. This is why wise parents focus solely on bonding and attachment during this stage, avoiding any concern over setting limits. Ideally, they do their best to consistently love their infants and extremely young children by soothing them when they cry and giving them everything they need. Every time they do, the cycle of trust is completed, and the parent-child relationship strengthens.

As our children approach and pass their first birthday, however, a different story begins to emerge. They become mobile, and they develop a large assortment of wants in addition to their needs. This is when it becomes imperative to begin exercising and strengthening our limit-setting muscle. Limits actually teach children how to share the love and respect they have been shown. Kids learn that the world does not revolve around them and that it's okay if they don't always get what they want. This, in turn, fosters humility and obedience, two virtues essential for spiritual growth.

While we continue to demonstrate great affection and compassion as we meet our children's needs, we must also begin to show them that they can't always have what they want. This is represented by another cycle that begins to spin around age one.

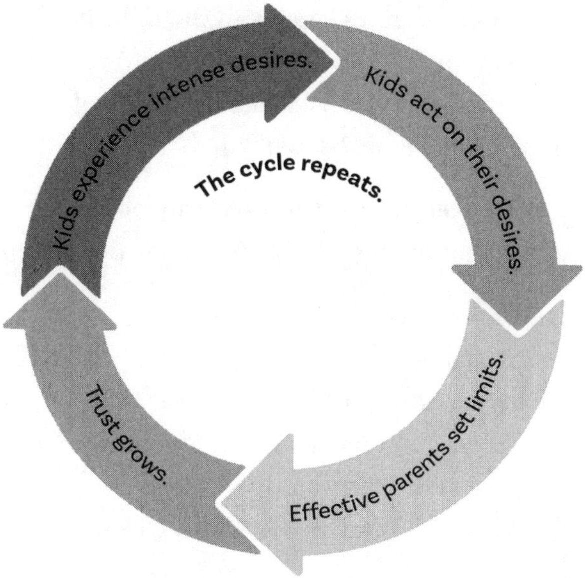

- **Kids experience an intense desire.** They want to grab the dog's tail and yank it. They want to bite their siblings. They want to run to and fro. They want to touch everything. They want a sample of this and a taste of that. They want and they want, rarely content with being still. Some of their desires are healthy. Others are not.
- **They act on their desires.** The human heart is prone to wander, being so frequently drawn to that which is attractive but cannot fulfill. Obviously, we shouldn't be surprised when our children act upon their desires. God gives us the freedom to make choices and to act upon them. He allows us to go after what we want so that we can learn through experience that apart from a relationship with Him there is only emptiness and pain.
- **Effective parents set limits on desires.** By doing so, we communicate three messages of love and commitment:
    - » I love you enough to keep you safe.

  - I love you enough to show you the right path.
  - I am so committed to your welfare and character that I will remain firm in my limits, regardless of how fiercely you try to make me back down.

- **Trust grows, leading to humility and obedience.** When we are steadfast and loving in our limits, our kids experience four truths essential to their walk with God:

  - I am loved and valuable, but my needs and desires are not more important than those of others.
  - Even if I don't get what I want, I trust that I will receive what I need.
  - There is someone far stronger and wiser than I who governs my life.
  - Because I am loved and safe, it's okay to submit to their authority and obey.

Christian parents are to do their best to set limits in strong and loving ways. In doing so, they seek to emulate Jesus Christ, the Creator and sustainer of the universe and our loving and compassionate Savior. He is the Lion and the Lamb. He is awesome in strength and love.

Considering this perspective on setting limits, let's return to Emily and the grocery store. Taking a deep breath to calm herself, she quickly took the snack from Sam, placed it back on the rack, and said gently but firmly, "Oh, this is sad. I know you want this, but you need to leave it alone." Then she moved the cart, with her daughter in it, just far enough so that the item was out of reach.

Samantha was not impressed with her mother's approach. With great gusto, she whined, "Candy . . . candy . . . candy!"

Emily held her ground, resisting the urge to lecture, threaten, rant, rave, or give in. Though she felt great embarrassment, she was comforted when she remembered that she had not entered the store that day with the purpose of building long-term relationships with her fellow shoppers or the store's employees. She was also comforted by the thought that pleasing God by raising a child who understands that no means no was more important than pleasing the masses.

On the way out to the car, Samantha's tears began to dry, and Emily sang the little song her mom had always sung to her: "I love you, sweet cheeks! I know God loves me too, because He gave me you!"

Again, God's strength is beyond comprehension, but so is His love. When we do our best to parent in ways that emulate these dual qualities of God's character, we give our children a glimpse of His glory. This is one of the most powerful ways we can help our children grow in spiritual strength.

Emily enforced the limit she set while demonstrating empathy and unwavering love for her daughter. The grace she showed was not confused with permissiveness. Instead, it was fulfilled by a commitment to do what was best for her daughter's character and spiritual strength in the long term. In parenting and all other relationships, it's important to remember that grace isn't about enabling bad behavior. It's about loving others enough to do what will benefit them most as they grow. When our children express unhappiness with limits, we enjoy the greatest odds of success when we remember this and do *not* fall into the trap of second-guessing ourselves—either by giving in or harshly demanding their obedience.

LIMITS FOR EVERY AGE, STAGE, AND PERSONALITY

Remember Joel and Abby? As they began to focus on fostering love and respect in their parenting—even on those stressful Sunday mornings—the tone of their relationships improved dramatically. There was still work to be done, however, especially when it came to setting limits. "Up until now," Abby told me, "I thought I was setting limits by lecturing and raising my voice. It seems like the problem Joel and I have is that we both talk a lot, but we don't really follow through on anything. I think a lot of this is because we just haven't known what to do."

It's one thing to understand the importance of setting limits. It's another thing to know how to set and hold to them!

From Ages One to Around Three

With young children, one to around three years, the limits we set should involve almost no words. Instead of complicating matters, we can calmly yet quickly do one of the following, depending on the situation:

- change our own location by moving away from our child;
- change the location of a problem object by taking it from our child;
- change our child's location by leading or carrying them someplace else.

Luke, Joel and Abby's two-year-old, had developed a habit of throwing a very loud fit anytime he didn't get what he wanted. Unless Luke was actively putting himself or someone else in physical danger, Joel and Abby learned that the most effective response usually involved calmly singing, "Uh-oh," and quickly moving themselves away from him. Singing this simple phrase allowed them to remain calm, demonstrating to Luke that he wouldn't get what he wanted by throwing a tantrum. Doing so also became a signal, helping this little one begin to understand when it was time for him to correct his behavior.

Abby started this approach one Sunday morning as she dropped him off at the children's ministry. As soon as they approached this area, he cried, "No, Mommy! I want you! Nooooo!"

Of course, Luke's cries pulled at Abby's heartstrings. She didn't want him to be upset—but she also knew it was important for him to grow in independence. In the past, she had given in and missed the service after attempting in vain to calm him down. This time was different. She simply changed her own location. With great love and respect in her voice, she sang, "Uh-oh," handed him over to Mrs. Romero, the children's care director, and quickly walked away.

When Abby returned after the service, Mrs. Romero smiled and whispered some words of encouragement. "I know leaving him like that was hard, but you did great. He calmed down right away. They often do when parents handle it like that. Good job."

Remember: Kids take their emotional cues from the adults around them. The calmer we are, the calmer they are likely to be.

That evening at home presented another opportunity for Abby and Joel to practice their new strategies. Luke decided to experiment with making a game of ramming his toy dump truck into the closed bathroom door while one of his sisters was using the potty. In the past, Joel had resorted to providing what Abby called mini psychotherapy sessions as he tried to gently teach Luke that his obnoxious behavior was upsetting others. Realizing that his talks weren't having the desired effect, Dad tried something new. "Uh-oh," he sang sweetly as he took the truck that Luke had been banging against the closed bathroom door and placed it out of reach. He, too, was starting to discover that handling things calmly with decisive action had far superior results than begging, pleading, or repeatedly trying to talk sense into a small child. Joel and Abby also saw that the simple "Uh-oh" song was becoming a signal to Luke that it was time for him to stop what he was doing. They really knew it was working when he immediately stopped trying to bite the dog after he heard his mother sing, "Uh-oh!" It was clear that Luke, even at age two, could learn that Scooter the poodle would have to go outside if he didn't treat her nicely.

Learning about this, many parents ask a wonderful question: "Should we use the 'Uh-oh' song right away, or should we first help our child understand that what they are doing is wrong?" Because it's always wise to err on the side of patience and good teaching, I recommend first teaching children that what they are doing is not okay. I also suggest showing them something they can do instead. For example, Joel and Abby had already taught little Luke that banging his toys against walls and biting the dog were not okay. They had also showed him how to play with his toys gently instead of roughly—and how to pet their poodle instead of biting her. What this couple also needed was permission to act in a loving yet decisive way when it became clear their son was not doing what he knew was right. There is a time for teaching, but there is also a time to show loving discipline through action.

With their newfound confidence, Joel and Abby decided to adapt the "Uh-oh" song to other situations where changing their location or removing an object didn't make sense. When appropriate, they began to change Luke's location, always keeping an eye on him and remaining calm. If you choose to do this, I recommend the following steps:

- **Sing, "Uh-oh," while leading or carrying your child to a safe spot.** Obviously, this strategy is to be used only for kids small enough to carry safely. Some parents place their child in a playpen where the child is in view but cannot get out. In public they might buckle their child into their shopping cart or stroller. The main consideration is that the location is safe.
- **Resist the urge to give in or talk too much.** When we give in to tantrums or other unacceptable behavior, we teach our kids to act this way more frequently. When we resort to using too many words, giving too much attention to unwanted behavior, our effectiveness diminishes as well.

- **While gently placing them in the safe spot, say, "I will let you come out when I see that you are calm."** From over three decades of professional and personal experience, I have found that the old rule of "one minute for every year of a child's age" is overly simplistic and rarely works well. A two- or three-year-old is rarely able to get themselves calmed down in only two or three minutes. If they are allowed to come out while they are still yelling, screaming, or misbehaving, we reward this undesirable behavior. Instead of making this mistake, allow your child to come out only after they have been reasonably calm for at least three to five consecutive minutes. This teaches self-control and patience, two incredibly important virtues.
- **Remain nearby, keeping an eye on your child while giving no attention to their misbehavior.** Understandably, many parents feel concerned when their child becomes emotional, cries, or yells because they want to be set free. Seeing one's child so upset can be heartbreaking, and some parents worry that if they don't try to soothe their child, it will damage the parent-child attachment relationship. This is not the case. Trying to calm them at this time will often lead them to becoming more upset for a longer period of time. It's also likely to reward their misbehavior and negative emotion.

  It's helpful to remember that what I am describing here represents only brief moments within the context of a much broader relationship full of love, respect, encouragement, attention, and joy. It's also important to note that the child is ultimately the one who decides whether they need to stay in the spot longer in order to calm down.

Recently, I consulted with an incredibly loving and attentive mom, Leslie, who was very concerned about using this approach. She was worried about causing her three-year-old daughter to feel abandoned; she always wanted her daughter to know how much she was loved. Leslie was an amazing mom, but she admitted that little Ella was becoming increasingly demanding and impatient: "I feel like she runs our home!"

After spending a great deal of time visiting and empathizing with Leslie, I suggested that she remember something: Over the past three years, she had already given Ella a strong foundation of love and affection. I also suggested she consider something else: Developmentally speaking, it was now time for Ella to see that she could be more independent and handle not being soothed every time she became upset.

Leslie replied, "I never thought of it that way. I want her to be more independent and to know that she will be okay when I'm not making her the center of things. She does need to start learning how to cope with uncomfortable emotions rather than always needing someone else to make her feel better."

"I agree, and I know she can handle this," I replied. "I also know you are an incredibly kind person who would never take this to extremes where she'd be neglected."

"No, never!" Leslie emphasized. "It's not like we are talking about hours here. It would be just a few minutes here and there."

"That's right," I agreed.

Three weeks later, Leslie shared a discovery she had made. "Now that I have been doing this consistently, Ella rarely has to go to her safe spot. I just have to sing, 'Uh-oh,' and she quickly settles down and behaves. Then we get to have fun together. It's amazing how well this worked when I decided to do it consistently without giving in or giving her so much attention when she was acting out. It definitely hasn't hurt our relationship either. Just the other day, I sang, 'Uh-oh,' and she immediately stopped acting out. As she did, she said, 'No. Mommy. I be with you.'"

As I hope you see, this approach is to be done with great love and firmness, never out of anger or with sarcasm. Our goal is to model the strength and love of God. To do it wisely, I find it helpful to continually pray the following:

> *Dear God, please give me the wisdom to parent my child with Your grace and truth. Help me know when it's best to soothe them and when it's best not to. Please help them learn to seek comfort from You rather than believing they can find it elsewhere.*

With this in mind, I offer these suggestions for responding to your child once they are ready to come out from the safe spot in which you have put them.

- **Avoid lecturing when they are ready to rejoin you.** Just give them a hug and say, "I love you." Some parents wonder if it is helpful to use this as a teachable moment—discussing with their child what they did wrong and how they might behave differently in the future. I counsel against this, as I have found through many years of practice that a short expression of love is far more powerful than a conversation about what the child should have done differently. I often wonder if this has to do with the unstated message we send when we simply provide a brief display of love instead: *I believe you are so capable of learning from the consequences of your actions that you don't need me to always tell you what you should learn from them.*

  I also believe that it is helpful for every parent to read and reread the parable of the prodigal son in Luke 15:11-32. In this amazing picture of the gospel, we see an account of a son who has gone astray and experienced many incredibly difficult consequences. When he chooses to return home, his father, who represents our heavenly Father, does not lecture or try to teach him a lesson. Instead, he runs to his son, hugging and kissing him.

  There is a time for everything. There is certainly a time for teaching our children to avoid making the same mistakes continually. My advice is to err on the side of doing such things when your children are calm, you are calm, and something upsetting has not just happened.

- **Repeat the process as needed.** Early in the training process, it's common for children to need multiple trips to their playpen, stroller, or other safe spot. The more consistent parents remain, the quicker children will grow to need this less. Some parents tell me they see dramatic improvement in less than three or four days. For others it takes longer. Some have even relayed that they have made quick progress, only to see their child backslide from time to time. Every child and every family is different, so please be patient with yourself and your kids. Also remember that this strategy is just one of many that wise and loving parents employ.

Joel and Abby first tried changing Luke's location one evening when he began teasing his siblings, grabbing at them, and generally acting like a terror. Without delay or any hesitation in his voice, Joel sang, "Uh-oh. It looks like you need a little away time."

Luke fell limp on the carpet, yelling, "No! Noooo!"

Joel calmly carried him to his playpen, which was set up within easy view. After gently setting Luke inside, he said, "You can come out when you are acting and sounding calm like me."

Luke just screamed, refusing to answer. Joel watched as his little boy tried to figure out how to climb out of the playpen. Taking a deep breath to stay calm, Joel prayed that God would give him wisdom to handle this situation well.

Fifteen minutes passed before Luke gained the composure to stop yelling and trying to force his way out. As he lifted Luke out of the playpen, Joel hugged him and said, "I love you, buddy." After that instance, Joel and Abby worked at being consistent: Anytime Luke acted out toward family members, Joel or Abby placed him in his playpen. They quickly began seeing improvement in his behavior; soon Luke responded to their "uh-oh" by settling down right away. Now he was spending much more time happily interacting with the family than crying in his playpen.

Age Three and Beyond

With youngsters between one and three, we can think about setting limits largely in terms of changing our location, the location of an object they are misusing, or their location. As these early years pass, however, wise parents realize that their kids are getting too big to carry safely, and they are also developing a more advanced ability to understand language. When we transition to conveying limits using our words, it's important to remember that God commands us to speak in pure and simple terms, sharing what we are completely able and committed to do: "Let what you say be simply 'Yes' or 'No'; anything more than this comes from evil" (Matthew 5:37).

Limits are promises to our children, so we need to ensure that we are capable of keeping them.

Limits are promises to our children, so we need to ensure that we are capable of keeping them. Because we cannot directly control the attitudes and behaviors of anyone else, our limits are 100 percent enforceable only when they focus on what *we* will do or allow. In other words, we set limits we can actually enforce. Which of the following fit into this category?

"Talk to me with a civil tone."	"I'll listen when your voice is calm."
"Pick up your toys."	"Feel free to keep the toys that you pick up."
"Hurry up."	"My car will be leaving for church at 7:30."

The statements in the left-hand column may sound good, but we cannot enforce them with absolute certainty. When we try to control the actions or attitudes of others, we often lose control. One mother shared, "As soon as I make the mistake of telling my daughter to talk to me in more civil ways, she starts to roll her eyes and get even more demanding or sarcastic. Then I'm totally powerless." Every time we tell a stubborn person what to do, we hand them our power.

The three statements in the right-hand column are actions you can control or impose. Because of this, they are enforceable statements.[1] The specific statements required in your home with your unique children will depend upon their age, ability, interests, and a variety of other factors. As you read the "Examples of Enforceable Statements for All Ages" list on pages 83–84, keep in mind that these are simply examples. Experiment with those that fit, and create others as needed.

Also, remember I have provided a long list only so you can see plenty of examples. Please don't post this on your refrigerator! Effective parents do not try to provide a lengthy assortment of limits. Instead, they stick with just the ones they need, adding others only as necessary. Because they are loving and positive leaders, they often have to set *fewer* limits than parents who are less effective in doing so. This is because they set limits within an overall context of love and respect, and they consistently enforce the limits that they do set.

A discussion of limits is not complete without mentioning that some kids need more than others, and some kids test them more than others. I have known many great parents who had at least one child who constantly seemed to challenge their authority. While this can be exhausting, it is not unusual. The good news is that it doesn't mean that this child is destined for big trouble. Many of the world's most amazing adults were children who habitually pushed against boundaries. If you have at least one strong-willed child, please take heart. With God's grace, you can do this!

Examples of Enforceable Statements for All Ages

- "I will listen when your voice sounds calm like mine."
- "We will stay at the park as long as you are not throwing sand."
- "You may be out of your stroller as long as you stay next to me and hold my hand."
- "I will give you your snack when I see that you have washed your hands."
- "I will play this game with you as long as you are not hitting me."
- "I read to kids who have their fingers out of their noses."
- "Feel free to join us for a snack as soon as you have picked up your toys."
- "When I see you throwing food, I know that you are done with your meal."
- "Breakfast is served until the timer on my phone rings. Feel free to eat what is served or wait until snack time."
- "My car leaves when the longer skinny hand on the clock gets to right here on the clock. That's thirty minutes from now. I'll also set the timer on the stove to buzz at that time."
- "I will help you with this as long as you are talking to me nicely."
- "I will help you with your school project as long as I feel that you are still working on it harder than I am."
- "I take kids to do fun things when I see that they have finished their chores."
- "I drive kids to places they want to go when they have proven they can ride in the car without arguing or fighting with each other."
- "I provide allowance one time per week."
- "I'm happy to pay half the cost of that new baseball bat."
- "Feel free to get online as long as I am here to supervise."
- "I allow kids to play sports as long as they are demonstrating good character."
- "Seth, Rebecca is welcome to come over as long as we are here."
- "I allow technology use in this home as long as the rules are being followed. No devices in bedrooms, devices are placed in my room at night, I have password access, and you cooperate with other things I ask of you."

- “I will allow you to drive the car when I see that you are being respectful and responsible about other matters.”
- “I’m happy to do extra things for you when I feel treated with respect and see that you are contributing to the family by helping with chores.”
- “I’m happy to help you pay for college as long as I see that you are keeping up your grades.”
- (To an adult child) “I’m happy to give you a place to live as long as I feel respected, you are contributing by helping out, and you are working hard to become self-supporting.”

The Value of Walking Away

Kurt was confounded. His son Todd had apparently concluded that becoming a teenager meant that he was no longer obligated to perform any duties around the house apart from basic personal hygiene and the maintenance of his computer gaming skills. Kurt had finally had enough when he asked his son to help clean the garage one Saturday. Glaring at Kurt, Todd said, "Dad, I shouldn't have to do any of this! Except for my bike, everything in the garage belongs to you. Anyway, you can't tell me what to do!"

Kurt felt so angry and hurt that he couldn't think. Because he'd studied the Love and Logic approach, he knew that sometimes it would be best to buy himself time rather than feel compelled to provide an immediate consequence. Taking this advice, he quietly yet very firmly told his son: "I'm going to have to do something about this, but I want to handle it well. I make better decisions when I'm calm. We'll talk then."

While it's always wise to resolve conflicts in relationships as quickly as possible, we usually make matters worse when we act before taking time to pray, seek guidance from others, and gain a calmer and more thoughtful perspective. Handling it in this way has the added benefit of modeling self-control and wisdom, two very important Christian virtues.

However, Todd was still angry. "Whatever!" he said.

In the past, Kurt often escalated conflicts with his son by arguing with him, making threats, or saying things he later regretted. This time was different. He simply walked away, praying for the strength to keep his cool.

Two days passed, during which time Kurt and his wife prayed for the strength to forgive their son while also holding him firmly accountable for his actions: "Oh, Lord, help us love Todd in ways that bring glory to You. Please give us the wisdom to raise a man who loves You with all his heart."

For those two days, Kurt and his wife took out the trash, emptied the dishwasher, fed the dogs, picked up the house, and vacuumed. The following day, Kurt approached his son a couple of hours before Todd planned to head to a classmate's house for a game night. "Todd, I've had some time to think about the other day when you yelled at me and told me that I couldn't tell you what to do."

Todd replied, "So? Why are you bringing that up now? That is in the past."

Kurt calmly continued: "Your mom and I love you too much to fight with you about getting your chores done. These things needed to be done, so we took care of them."

A bit confused, Todd inquired, "Okay, so what's the problem?"

Kurt explained with sincere empathy, "The sad news is that we provide use of the computer, rides to and from your friends' houses and practice, and other luxuries when we see that you are being respectful, responsible, and pleasant to be around."

"Wait—what about tonight? You need to drive me to Ryan's house. I told him I'd be over!" Todd yelled.

Seeing the sad but determined look on his dad's face, Todd continued, "This is so unfair! Why do you think that you can just boss me around anytime you want?"

Resisting the temptation to argue, Kurt said with empathy, "I know that being a teenager is not easy, but we love you too much to argue about these things."

Todd countered, "But this is stupid!"

While walking away, Kurt calmly repeated, "We love you too much to argue."

When we allow ourselves to get pulled into angry interchanges and arguments with our children, what are the chances we still appear strong and loving in their eyes? As soon as we become frustrated and angry, we forfeit our authority as parents. As soon as our veins begin to bulge and the volume of our voice increases, it becomes clear to a kid that they can control our emotions and our behavior.

PRACTICE SESSIONS ARE ESSENTIAL

Let's return to Joel and Abby. Love and respect were growing in their home, but one problem still seemed insurmountable: the Sunday-morning scramble.

As they prayed about this struggle, Joel and Abby were struck by the fact that God does not simply lay down rules, walk away, and then expect us to know how to follow them. Rather, He teaches and empowers. He gives us His Word, full of instruction and packed with examples. He counsels us with His Holy Spirit, enabling us to learn how to live according to His will. He gives us what we need to succeed.

When we set limits as consultant parents, we are wise to teach our children how to abide by them. Joel and Abby decided that the best way to help their children learn to be successful on Sunday morning was to teach them one Friday evening and then have a practice session on Saturday morning. As they prepared, they listed all the things that they needed to show their children how to do:

- After dinner on Friday we can help them learn how to set their alarm clocks and choose their outfits for church. We will show them how to gather everything they will need for the morning and put it together in one spot.
- Saturday morning, we'll show them how to get themselves dressed, do their hair, grab something to eat for breakfast, and clean up after themselves as they do.

Friday evening, Joel and Abby gathered the kids together and explained their plan. Joel took the lead. "I have some really good news for all of you!" he said with excitement and a smile.

Six-year-old Becky immediately piped up, "What, Daddy? What is the good news?"

Joel continued, "All of you, except Chloe, are big enough now to get yourselves ready in the mornings without needing Mom and me to treat you like little kids."

Thirteen-year-old Madison rolled her eyes and argued, "But Luke won't know what to do."

"No worries," Abby answered. "Your dad and I will give all of you some ideas tonight, and we'll practice tomorrow morning by getting ready to leave for Grandma and Grandpa's house by 7:30. We'll be here to help, but we're sure that you are going to do great."

Madison countered, "Yeah, but what if we still aren't ready to go on Sunday morning?"

Continuing to smile, Joel answered, "That might happen, but it's no big deal. Our car will still be leaving for church at 7:30."

"What if we aren't dressed by then?" she continued to press.

Without a hint of frustration or sarcasm, Abby replied, "No problem. The car will still be leaving at 7:30, and we'll all be in it, ready or not. We'll practice tomorrow."

Joel and Abby showed each of the kids how to gather what they needed for the next day and how to set their alarm clocks. In the morning, they practiced the entire process, leaving for their grandparents' house by 7:30.

WHY IT'S WISE TO WELCOME MISTAKES

The central virtue is love. All others flow from it. Loving our kids well requires that we first remember our own faults, frailties, and need for grace. It requires admitting that our own maturation has come largely as a result of making plenty of mistakes. The most fortunate people are allowed to make plenty of small ones early in life when the consequences are still small. The freedom to experience these low-cost learning experiences is truly a blessing. When children are given this gift, they are far more likely to grow in love and respect for their parents rather than becoming mired in rebellion. They also find it far easier to love others as themselves.

> The most fortunate people are allowed to make plenty of small mistakes early in life when the consequences are still small.

Back to Joel and Abby's story: Sunday came—it was game time. Just as God does for us, Joel and Abby guided when guidance was needed while still allowing each child the freedom to learn through experience. Instead of resorting to anger, lectures, and threats, or trying to do everything for the kids, they simply said, "The car is leaving at 7:30. We set the timer on the stove to go off ten minutes before that."

Madison was the first to complain. "I can't find my brush. My hair is all tangled!"

Abby calmly replied, "I will help you with it as soon as I am ready to go."

Impatient, Madison replied, "I guess I have to do everything around here" and quickly found another brush to drag through her hair.

The next to have a problem was little Luke. "Daddy! Shirt stuck!"

"That's okay," Joel answered. As Joel helped Luke pull his shirt over his shoulders, Joel remembered to involve his son in the process as much as possible. He told Luke, "I bet you can put your pants on. Show me how you do it."

Standing, Luke put his feet into his pants and tried to pull them up. "Stuck, Daddy!" He frowned.

Joel smiled and said, "That's okay. Let me show you how to put them on lying down."

Luke giggled as his daddy helped him.

Madison screamed from the other room, "I'm going to be late! I hate these clothes!"

Both Joel and Abby wisely chose to listen and empathize rather than trying to address this problem. "That's got to be frustrating," Abby replied with sincerity.

When the timer on the kitchen stove eventually buzzed, the kids were in varied states of readiness. Nevertheless, Joel and Abby stuck to the promise they had made. By 7:30, their car left the driveway, headed toward church. Luke had grape juice stains around his mouth. Madison's hair looked like a rat's nest. Becky's jacket was on inside out.

Despite the imperfections, it was evident to Joel and Abby that they were making major progress. The biggest change was in their own behavior, and they knew that in the long run, that was all they could truly control. God would do the rest as they played their role by parenting with love and strength.

CHAPTER 5

THE GIFT OF DISCIPLINE

Promoting Honesty and Accountability

Ava breathed a sigh of relief when she heard the sound of the lawn mower. "Finally, he's doing it," she whispered to herself.

The sweet music of fourteen-year-old Max mowing the lawn was suddenly replaced with silence and the sound of him trudging through the back door. "Mom?" he called. "The lawn mower stopped working."

"What's wrong with it?" she asked.

"It just stopped. It won't restart," he replied flatly.

"Well, did you try to figure out how to get it going again?"

"It's not my fault! I can't get it started because it's a piece of junk," Max complained.

"Dad said something about making sure that it had enough oil or the engine would be ruined. I remember him showing you how to check that and saying you needed to do so every time you used it," Ava replied as she led her son back outside to look.

Moving at a snail's pace, Max trudged out the door to check the oil. The dipstick was dry.

Frustrated beyond words, Ava raised her voice. "I heard Dad tell you many times that the engine would be ruined if it ran out of oil!"

"I did check it. It's not my fault!" Max said. "It's just junk anyway!"

That evening, Edwin returned from a business trip. Exhausted, he was looking forward to a relaxing evening with his loving family. Instead, he was barraged by conflicting reports about what had happened.

Over dinner Ava vented. "I've got bad news. The mower stopped working today. Max hasn't been checking the oil."

Max countered, "It's not my fault. That thing is so old. Why do I always get blamed for everything?"

Without thinking, Edwin growled, "Oh, for crying out loud, Max! I have talked with you about this so many times. I showed you how to check the oil level, and I even watched you to be sure you felt comfortable doing it. It doesn't take more than a minute or two to check and see if it's filled up! Why can't you just do what I tell you to do? Why do you have to lie about it?"

The next day, a small-engine mechanic confirmed the grim diagnosis. "It looks like your mower's been low on oil for quite a while. That's too bad, because it would have lasted for at least two more years if you'd kept it filled. That's why it's a good habit to check it every time you use it. We can fix it, but it'll be cheaper for you to buy a new one."

Ava and Edwin came to see me because they were concerned that Max had slipped into the habit of "forgetting" to do what he was told. "It's not my fault" and "I can't __________ because __________" were some of his favorite phrases.

In an early session, they told me about the lawn mower incident that had happened a few days earlier. "Max is a good student, and his teachers have always said what a great kid he is," Ava told me. "But we've noticed at home that he's begun to make excuses to try to get out of chores—particularly when he wants to go play soccer with his friends. Part of this pattern is him acting like we haven't taught him how to do something that we've actually spent a large amount of time making sure that he could.

"For example, I have repeatedly shown him how to load the dishwasher so that drinking glasses don't hit against each other and get broken. He keeps being careless and slamming them in. Then he lies when another glass comes out cracked. What bothers me most is when we repeatedly catch him in the same lies."

Like the sound of a fluorescent light fixture humming in the background, Max's dual habits of dishonesty and lack of personal accountability were becoming increasingly annoying. Not only that, but Edwin and Ava realized that if they weren't addressed now, the consequences could become more serious once Max was older.

LOVING DISCIPLINE: THE DOORWAY TO HONESTY AND ACCOUNTABILITY

As we've seen, setting and enforcing limits is key to our children developing godly virtues such as love, respect, humility, and obedience. In this chapter, you will discover how to help your children grow in two additional aspects of spiritual strength: honesty and accountability. Both are essential to learning personal responsibility.

God's plan to shape the lives of us and our children includes discipline. He knows that sometimes we must experience great discomfort, even pain, so that we can bear fruit and experience peace. Because He loves us, He is willing to discipline us: "For the moment all discipline seems painful rather than pleasant, but later it yields the peaceful fruit of righteousness to those who have been trained by it" (Hebrews 12:11).

What Is Discipline?

What comes to mind when you hear the word *discipline*? In the English language, this word has become primarily associated with attempts to control behavior through punishment involving physical or mental pain. The Greek word *paideia* used in Hebrews 12:11 refers to discipline, but it has a much broader meaning than we might assume. Instead of narrowly reflecting the practice of punishment and control, it includes instruction, guidance, and correction in moral and spiritual matters.

According to this more comprehensive understanding, it is clear that we discipline our children in a variety of ways, including

- teaching them God's Word;
- providing a godly example;
- letting them experience struggles;
- allowing them to make choices and learn from the consequences;
- correcting them when they persist in wrong attitudes and actions;
- coming alongside them when necessary to help them learn from their mistakes; and
- repeatedly doing all the above over many years.

Sometimes discipline results in uncomfortable or even painful feelings for our kids, but we discipline with the purpose of preventing even greater pain. God is both compassionate and just, both loving and powerful, both graceful and full of truth, and the way we discipline our children should reflect these qualities as much as possible.

Discipline is most effective within the context of a loving and respectful relationship. The greater the love and respect in the relationship with our kids, the harder it will be for them to blame us when we provide discipline. Instead, they will be more likely to see that their poor decisions are the source of their discomfort and pain.

Before we talk further about discipline, I want to briefly address the subject of corporal punishment. Some Christians have heard that if they "spare the rod, they will spoil the child" (see Proverbs 13:24). There is much debate regarding the true meaning of *rod*. I recognize that I am not the ultimate and final authority on parenting. God is. I would, however, like to share my opinion. Based on my study of the entirety of Scripture, I do *not* believe that the rod represents a physical object used to spank, hit, or whip. When we seek to punish merely with the intent of achieving power by imposing physical pain, our children are unlikely to take full responsibility for their actions. Instead, they will likely grow to resent us and blame us for their problems.

I believe that the rod mentioned in Proverbs 13 represents the shepherd's staff, or *shevet*, which was used as a symbol of authority as well as a tool for guidance, correction, and leadership. David referred to this rod in what is probably the best-known psalm:

> Though I walk through the valley of the shadow of death,
> I will fear no evil,
> for you are with me;
> your rod and your staff,
> they comfort me.
>
> **PSALM 23:4**

Sheep scatter when they are struck, but they follow when they are guided, protected, and cared for.

DISCIPLINING SO OUR KIDS WILL FOLLOW RATHER THAN SCATTER

Never before have parents been more conflicted about the role of discipline in raising kids. At the heart of these concerns is the desire to correct without ruining their relationship with their children. Out of fear, many modern parents rely entirely on praise, encouragement, and constant rescuing to teach their children. As we learned in earlier chapters, chronic helicopter and permissive parenting often leads to chronically unhappy and irresponsible kids who are ill-prepared for adulthood. Because these parents exercise little or no loving authority, their children see no need to follow them.

Drill sergeant parents fall at the other end of the spectrum. They believe that discipline requires them to raise their voices and demonstrate anger or sarcasm over their children's poor decisions. Somehow many such parents have come to believe that this is how to raise children with honest and accountable hearts.

Imagine you have a boss at work who is not pleased with a mistake you made. How would you respond if your supervisor yelled, "This sort of thing makes me so mad! Why did I ever give you this responsibility in the first place? You need to redo this report and get it on my desk by tomorrow morning! I hope you give some long and hard thought to your level of commitment to the team"?

Would you be thinking more about your role in the problem, or about how badly you were being treated? Would you be experiencing the logical consequences of your mistake, or would you primarily feel hurt, anger, or resentment? Would you be inspired to follow your manager or find another job?

Drill sergeant parents make themselves an easy target for blame in the hearts of their children. By displaying anger and frustration, they unwittingly offer themselves as scapegoats for the problem. Because our sinful human nature already primes us to deflect responsibility, parents should not be surprised when their expressions of anger and hurt make children grow more resentful—and often sneaky—rather than truly responsible.

Now let's imagine that you have a boss who operates like a consultant parent. With sincere empathy, this person demonstrates concern while still expecting you to correct your mistake: "It's never pleasant to find out something like this. There are a number of errors in this report. I wish I didn't have to share this bad news, but I need you to get it fixed and back to me by tomorrow morning. That's when I have to share it with the owners."

In this situation, would you still be upset? Probably. Because of your boss's empathy, what would you be the most upset about? The manager's actions or yours?

> We can offer our kids compassion even as we allow them to face the discomfort or pain associated with their poor decisions.

Central to the Christian faith is the truth that God acted first: We love because He first loved us; Christ died for us while we were still sinners; we have faith only through the grace He first gave. In parenting, we help our children mature when we go first by providing empathy even when we don't think our kids deserve it. By giving them grace, we help them experience our love and compassion as we simultaneously allow them to face the discomfort or pain associated with their poor decisions. Grace and discipline (love and strength) go hand in hand. Notice the responses to anger versus empathy:

Our anger gives kids a reason to be upset with us.
Our empathy allows them to be upset
with their own poor decisions.

When your child's poor decision-making leads to consequences, you may find it difficult to convey empathy. The examples on page 99 may help. You can pick just one from the list, taking care to select a

Q & A: What Should You Do When Your Kids Act Disrespectfully Toward You?

Young people who've learned to demonstrate respect to their parents lead far happier and more productive lives than those who do not. This fact even shows up as a promise in the middle of God's Ten Commandments: "Honor your father and your mother, that your days may be long in the land that the LORD your God is giving you" (Exodus 20:12).

One of the most important ways to teach kids to respect and love God is by teaching them to respect and love you. This is why the following steps are so important.

- **Treat your kids with great love and respect so they will know how to treat you.** Great leaders model the behavior they desire from others. The Good Shepherd leads us in paths of righteousness. He does not prod us from behind, constantly demanding that we rise to a standard that He is unwilling to demonstrate.
- **When your kids are disrespectful, do your best to avoid taking it personally.** When parents allow their children's arguing, complaining, and other forms of disrespect to get under their emotional skin, it teaches kids that they can control their parents' emotions. The angrier or more frustrated and hurt these parents act, the more disrespectful their children behave.
- **Calmly describe what you will do or allow, using very few words.** Instead of getting emotional, set very concise limits. Examples include:
    - "I provide privileges and do extra things for people when they treat me with respect."
    - "When I hear arguing, my answer is always no."
    - "I will listen when your tone is calm and respectful."
- **Enforce these limits without anger, lectures, threats, or repeated warnings.** Our children often demonstrate disrespect when they are beginning to feel insecure about whether we are strong enough and loving enough to give them the discipline they need. When we show a consistent willingness to enforce the limits we have set, they tend to be far happier and pleasant to be around.

phrase that you can say with sincerity. Change it a bit if you need to. Pray over it and consider the great empathy God has lavished upon you. As you do, you'll start to feel your attitude toward your child's mistakes and misbehaviors soften. When it does, your expression of empathy will become more natural and authentic.

"I can't imagine how [fill in the feeling] this must be."
"Oh, no. These sorts of things are so upsetting."
"I'm feeling for you."
"This is so sad."
"That's never good."
"It looks like you are feeling really [fill in the feeling]."
"Do you want a hug?"
"I bet this hurts."

MAX RECEIVES A GIFT

About a week after Max's lawn mower mishap, I asked Edwin and Ava what they had decided to do about the problem.

Edwin hesitated. "Well, I've been stalling. I just don't want to be mean about this."

I nodded and said, "It's never good to be mean." Then I said bluntly: "But is it unreasonable or mean to provide the type of discipline that will save your son from future pain?"

Edwin slowly shook his head. "No, it isn't. I know I need to talk with him about it as soon as possible, and I know that he needs to experience a consequence for being careless and then lying about it."

"That would be a gift to him," I agreed.

The following day, Edwin approached his son and said, "We need to talk."

"About what?" Max asked.

Edwin sat next to him, placing his hand gently on his son's shoulder. "Son," he replied with empathy, "this whole thing about the lawn mower is very sad. I can't imagine how upsetting it must have been when you realized that you'd let it run out of oil."

Jerking away from his father, Max replied, "I told you guys that it wasn't my fault!"

Although anxious and upset inside, Edwin maintained a calm and concerned tone. "Max, I love you too much to argue about this. The new mower cost $320. It just makes sense that you make things right."

Shocked, Max yelled, "I shouldn't have to pay for a new one!"

Edwin answered calmly. "I agree, but I do expect you to pay for two years of the cost since the mechanic said our mower should have lasted that much longer."

Max looked slightly relieved but still a bit panicked. "How much will that be?"

Edwin continued, "I found out that the average push mower lasts eight years, so two years of value comes to eighty dollars."

"I have to give you eighty bucks?" Max said, his eyes wide. "Where am I supposed to get that kind of money?"

Edwin replied kindly but firmly, "I'm not sure how you will earn the money, but I know that you will figure this out. If you want to bounce some ideas around on how to do that, just let me know."

THE "PRICE TAGS" GO UP EVERY DAY

As I reflect on Edwin and Ava's journey with their son, I'm thankful that God gave them a sense of urgency regarding the importance of providing firm yet loving discipline. Max continued to sulk for a day or so after his talk with Edwin. Then over dinner the following Monday, he said, "My friend Tony told me that his neighbor gave him twenty dollars for raking her leaves on Saturday. Do you think anyone on our street might hire me to do yard work?"

Edwin put down his fork and smiled. He and Max began brainstorming about people they knew who might gladly pay someone to help in their yard. From this experience, Max learned that being conscientious and truthful is less costly than evading accountability and lying about it. He also learned that earning eighty dollars requires doing a lot of tiring yard work around the neighborhood.

Shading the truth and avoiding accountability may seem to have relatively small consequences when our children are young, but the price tag goes up every day. Lying or making excuses about taking a cookie from the cookie jar, pulling a sibling's hair, or failing to take out the trash very easily grows into believing that there's no need to be honest and accountable to anyone else, including God.

Because the costs incurred by poor character rise with "inflation" as our kids get older, doesn't it make sense that we do everything within our power to help our kids avoid being in debt to it? As you'll see, teaching your kids honesty and accountability requires much more than disciplining them when they've stumbled. Let's look at four proactive parenting practices that dramatically increase the odds that your children will learn to face life with integrity and the courage required to humbly hold themselves accountable:

1. Show your kids what honesty and accountability *really* look like.
2. Allow them to practice by making choices within limits.
3. Let empathy and consequences do the teaching.
4. Let them see that you believe in them.

Show What Honesty and Accountability *Really* Look Like

As I worked with Ava and Edwin, I noticed that, not only were they quite concerned about ensuring that their son lived with integrity, but they were also conscientious Christians hindered by fears of not measuring up. They believed that God loved them and that He forgave them when they confessed their own shortcomings, but they were afraid to truly live that way. Trying to manage their pain, they just worked harder trying to be perfect each and every day. The results were more feelings of shame and higher perfectionistic standards for themselves. The resulting exhaustion was robbing them of the strength they needed to truly hold their son accountable.

Perhaps you relate to Ava and Edwin's feelings—or perhaps you wonder why anyone would be so hard on themselves. Either way, since you've read this far, I'm guessing you place a huge value on showing your kids what godliness looks like. You probably already know the importance of your children seeing you reading God's Word, serving others, being patient, refraining from the use of four-letter words, extending love and forgiveness, being responsible, providing for your family, driving the speed limit, seeking peace, resisting materialism, dressing modestly, and doing the many other things that "good Christians" do. These are great behaviors, but the odds are high that you are already working hard at them.

When we focus on our failures, we are more likely to model anxiety and shame than the great freedom and grace offered by Christ.

Here's the real challenge: Regardless of how hard we try, there will be times when our kids witness us falling short. No parent, even the most faithful Christian, has the ability to display perfect behavior in front of their kids all the time, particularly when facing serious challenges with work, finances, marriage, health, and other stressors. In fact, if we become discouraged, or dwell in shame over making mistakes, we will fail more often. How ironic! *When we focus on our failures, we are more likely to model anxiety and shame than the great freedom and grace offered by Christ.*

God wants to give us freedom. This is not freedom from responsibility. It's the freedom required to be real as we struggle to grow in Christ and do what is right. A constant theme embedded throughout this book is this: One of the primary ways God enables us to grow is by allowing us to make mistakes and experience the consequences.

For the deeply conscientious Christian, the most painful realization is that we have not lived up to the standard set by Christ, the One who loves us so much that He gave His life for us. We see Peter grappling with such pain when he realized that fear had compelled him to deny Christ three times: "The Lord turned and looked at Peter. And Peter remembered the saying of the Lord, how he had said to him, 'Before the rooster crows today, you will deny me three times.' And he went out and wept bitterly" (Luke 22:61-62).

Christ's love, kindness, and patience lead us to repentance (see Romans 2:4). If we were not free to slip up, would we have such a great glimpse of His incomprehensible love?

When we place ourselves in chains of self-condemnation, our children notice—and may follow our lead. Decades ago, I began to witness a common pattern in many of the most conscientious families that led to two unfortunate outcomes. First, parents who work extremely hard to be perfect often unintentionally teach their kids that assuming responsibility makes people desperately unhappy. One boy said it well: "Yeah, my parents have to work really hard and be responsible all the time to be so miserable. Count me out."

Second, because of the perfectionistic standards unintentionally modeled by these parents, their children often learn to deny and deceive out of fear that they will not measure up. Their primary goal becomes looking good in the eyes of others rather than truly growing in their relationship with God.

The freedom to be authentic and embrace accountability comes when we accept the loving grace of God and trust that He will use both our strengths and imperfections to bring Him glory. Max desperately needed to see his parents admit when they fell short and depended on God's grace. Every child needs to see this! Because of this I gave Edwin and Ava some simple yet powerful strategies to experiment with. Regardless of your child's age or maturity, I pray that you will try them as well.

1. **As often as possible, show your children that it's okay to make mistakes.** Intentionally allow your kids to see you making small mistakes. You might admit when you burned part of dinner, wore two slightly different colored socks, drove past an exit on the highway, or mispronounced a word. As you do, allow them to see you laugh a bit about these errors rather than becoming defensive, angry, or self-critical.

2. **Let them overhear you talking about what you are learning.** Isn't it interesting that our children often pay closer attention to what they overhear us saying than what we try to tell them directly? Because of this, let your kids listen as you tell a friend or your spouse about what you are learning from the small mistakes you make. This reinforces the fact that mistakes are learning opportunities. It also models humility and truthfulness.

   For example, over dinner they might overhear you telling your spouse: "Honey, I learned something today. I learned that when I get in a hurry, I might miss the No Parking sign on a street and get a parking ticket. The good thing about life is that we are always learning something new."

3. **Use Scripture to show them that God loves the honest and humble.** Read the parables of the tax collector and the Pharisee (see Luke 18:9-14) and the prodigal son (see Luke 15:11-32) with your kids to show them that God forgives those who confess their sins rather than those who try to look "cool" or who boast about how good they are. Then I encourage you to read and talk about the meaning of Hebrews 4:15: "For we do not have a high priest who is unable to sympathize with our weaknesses, but one who in every respect has been tempted as we are, yet without sin." As you discuss that

Christ is our compassionate Redeemer, pray together, thanking God for His grace and asking Him to help you grow from the truth embedded in these powerful examples.

Allow Them to Practice by Making Choices Within Limits

Our heavenly Father is sovereign. Nothing falls beyond His control. For the sake of His name, however, He allows us freedom within the boundaries He has established. The growth we experience by making choices can bring Him glory and benefit us tremendously. Our children can also profit when we allow them to make plenty of small choices within the limits we set. A side effect is that we tend to experience far fewer control battles.

In addition to modeling the freedom to make mistakes and learn, Edwin and Ava needed to allow Max to start making as many small choices as possible. I described the concept by sharing a story about Jon, a middle school math teacher who was well-acquainted with getting the best from kids. I once asked him, "So, Jon, how do you do it? How do you keep things running so smoothly while at the same time building responsibility in your students?"

"I give them a ton of little choices," he replied, "to cut down on power struggles and teach them responsibility."

"So how did you get started?" I asked. "What did you do first?"

"I began by giving them a math assignment with twice as many problems as I wanted them to complete. Then I gave them a choice: 'Are you going to do the odd ones or the even ones? You decide.'"

"Did it work?" I asked.

"It confused the daylights out of them," he said, smiling. "They were so busy deciding which ones they were going to do that they didn't have much time to complain about having to do so many."

"Nice!" I chuckled.

"Yeah, and the next day I asked them whether they were going to show their work on the front or the back of their page. The day after that I gave them two worksheets. One was on white paper and the other on yellow. Then I told them, 'You can choose whether to complete the yellow sheet or the white one first. You decide.'"

I replied, "How'd that day go?"

Jon laughed. "Even though the choices were small, they still made a big difference. It just shows how badly most people want freedom. One of the kids joked with me a bit, 'Hey! You're gonna make us crazy with all these choices!'"

"Did the situation improve?" I asked.

"It did, but it was messy too," Jon answered. "It was all rainbows and unicorns until they started complaining about the choices I was giving. One of them even said something like 'What if we choose not to choose?'"

"How did you handle that?" I asked.

"The next day I didn't give them any choices. I wasn't mean; I just told them, 'I need the entire worksheet completed with answers provided on the front next to each problem.'"

"I bet they didn't like that," I said.

Jon shook his head. "Nope. When they complained about it, I said very nicely, 'I give choices as long as there is no arguing over them. When there is, I make the choices.' Then I waited a couple of days and started giving options again after their attitudes improved."

"So," I reflected, "they learned that the more respectful and responsible they behaved, the more freedom they were able to enjoy. This isn't just about making your job easier but about helping kids grow in character."

"Exactly!" Jon answered. "It helps teach kids that the quality of their choices matters. I think God handles us this way a lot of the time. He gives us freedom but also allows us to see how we can lose it through our own sin and rebellion. Then He gives us grace, and we start learning all over again."

A number of questions may be popping into your mind right

now: *What does this have to do with parenting? I can see how this might work in a classroom with middle school students, but what types of choices might I give my kids? How young can I start?*

Listed below are some examples of choices given by parents of kids in all stages—from toddlerhood to adolescence. As you read, notice that each choice provides just two options, both acceptable to the parent. Also remember that these are simply examples. As the parent, you get to decide the choices you ultimately provide to your kids.

- "Will you be having your milk in your red cup or your blue one?"
- "You may hold my hand in the parking lot or stay in your stroller. You decide."
- "Do you want to brush your top teeth or your bottom teeth first?"
- "Will you be putting your shirt on first or your shorts on first?"
- "How do you want to get into your car seat? Do you want to climb in or have me put you in?"
- "Breakfast is served until the timer on the stove buzzes. Are you going to eat what is served or wait until lunch?"
- "Will you be doing your homework first or your chores first?"
- "Are you going to bed now or in fifteen minutes?"
- "The church is requesting help with vacation Bible school and building maintenance. Which one of these will you be signing up for this summer?"
- "You may participate in one sport this spring. I know you like both baseball and soccer. Which one of these will you choose?"
- "Will you be paying your car insurance with cash or by doing extra jobs around the house?"

As you read this list, you may be wondering, *What if my child refuses to decide, chooses an alternative that I didn't offer, complains about the choices I give, or wants to make choices over issues that I need to make the decision on?* Like the decisions God allows us to make, the choices we give our children are governed by loving yet firm limits. We provide these boundaries as we follow the rules listed below:

- Remember to provide two options, each of which you'll be happy with.
- Give most of your choices when your child is behaving well. Give very few when they aren't.
- Give choices only when your child decides quickly without arguing or complaining.
- Never give choices when a child demands them.
- Remember that the primary purpose of giving choices is so that your children will learn how to make them and to live with the consequences in an honest and accountable manner.

Edwin and Ava started seeing the connection between giving choices within limits and helping Max learn to become more honest and responsible. They started giving ones like, "Will you be mowing the lawn this week or trimming the hedges?" "Are you going to wash the glasses by hand or place them in the dishwasher far enough apart that they won't hit each other?" "You can decide whether to take the dog for a walk each night this week, or you can commit to doing it next week."

Edwin surmised, "It's like we're starting with milk rather than solid food. Max needs practice seeing that his choices really matter. This is a safe way for him to get it."

"That's a good way to think about it," I answered. "We give these small choices so that our kids will learn to make honest and accountable decisions with bigger choices."

On that note, I told Edwin and Ava another story from my friend Jon. His wife, Julie, began offering their daughter, Amy, small choices when she was in kindergarten. Amy had fought every morning as her mom got her ready for school, so Julie decided to stop trying to force her to eat breakfast. Instead, she gave her a choice between two small items and let her decide how much she needed to eat. Then, instead of insisting that Amy wear what she wanted her to, Julie let her decide between two different outfits she'd laid out ahead of time. Julie also didn't fight with her about her hair. She just asked her if she wanted to fix it herself or wanted some help.

"How did that work out?" Ava asked.

I explained that Amy once came to breakfast wearing several mismatched barrettes and a headband, and she didn't eat more than a mouthful of cereal. Because the weather had started getting cold, Julie asked her whether she wanted to wear her jacket or carry it. Amy wouldn't put it on, but she did put it next to her as her mom buckled her into her car seat.

On their drive, Amy complained about feeling chilly. Julie turned up the heat a bit but not enough to make it super comfortable. She made sure Amy wasn't shivering, but the little girl still complained about feeling cold. Instead of getting mad and lecturing her daughter, Julie silently thanked God for providing this learning experience. This made it easier for her to empathize with Amy: "I know that it's really hard to feel cold. I love you" is all that Julie said.

Within a few days, Amy ate more breakfast and even asked whether it was cold outside. She and Julie looked at the thermometer together, and Amy decided when it would be best for her to wear her coat rather than carry it.

"She learned to choose well when Julie allowed her the freedom to do so," Edwin noted.

"Yep," I said. "The price tag of poor decisions goes up every day. I think Amy learned a lot more than the importance of wearing her coat."

Edwin and Ava also began to have some fun with this simple strategy, noticing that Max was a bit less resistant when they asked him to help around the house. "Max," Edwin asked, "are you going to empty the dishwasher now or just have it done before I take you to basketball practice?"

Max was quick to answer. "Not now! I'm busy."

Edwin replied, "No problem."

An hour later, Max approached his father, saying, "It's time to go to practice. We need to leave now."

Edwin replied with empathy, "That's really unfortunate. We'll get going just as soon as the dishwasher is emptied."

Let Empathy and Consequences Do the Teaching

Beginning with the broken lawn mower, Edwin and Ava learned to discipline their son without losing his love and respect. They discovered that allowing Max to experience natural consequences with empathy and compassion was far more effective than providing consequences with anger, lectures, or threats. Their goal was to help their son become more unhappy with his poor decision than he was with them. That's when real honesty and accountability are learned. That is why Edwin didn't display anger over the dishwasher not being emptied. Instead, he quickly empathized, resisted the urge to lecture, and allowed Max to learn from the consequence of arriving late to practice.

> Allowing our kids to experience natural consequences with empathy and compassion is far more effective than providing consequences with anger, lectures, or threats.

I remember very fondly how my parents, who were both first-class drill sergeant parents when I was young, began to learn the importance of empathy rather than anger. Perhaps the biggest hurdle they had to overcome was believing that being empathetic meant being permissive. As soon as they discovered that they could be loving while also holding me firmly accountable, my relationship with them dramatically improved. I no longer needed to lie about what I had done or fight with them about the consequences. By the time I was old enough to get my driver's license, we were having almost no protracted arguments or power struggles.

Around this time, I decided I wanted a car. My father blessed me by allowing me to have any year and model I wanted as long as I could find the money to pay for it. As you might imagine, this forced me to rely primarily on the school bus, rides from family and friends, and occasional use of my dad's rusty old GMC pickup for transportation. But I was also motivated to work as many odd jobs as possible and save my pennies. After a year and a half, I'd put away enough to buy a car that had been sitting in a neighbor's yard for quite a while with a faded "For Sale" sign taped to the inside of the windshield. Because I was seventeen, I lacked the maturity to question the wisdom of buying a car nobody else wanted.

The brakes created a slight slowing effect, the steering was loose, the tires had little tread, and the motor smoked. Before I could do much driving at all, I needed to do work on the vehicle. I made an age-related decision: The first improvement needed to be a new stereo. I still had enough extra cash to make this purchase. The other "small" mechanical issues could wait.

When my mom saw me grab my car keys one Saturday, she asked, "Where are you heading off to? It looks like you are in a hurry."

"I'm heading to town to get some parts for my car," I answered.

Cheerfully she asked, "What are you getting?"

"A stereo. That old radio stinks," I answered.

With a look of loving concern, she replied, "Would you like my thoughts on that?"

I'd already made my mind up, but I figured it would be rude if I didn't let her share. "What?" I asked.

With that same look of gentle concern, she answered, "I'd be worried that if I spent the money on a stereo, I wouldn't have any left to fix something else that might go wrong."

"Nothing else is going to break," I quickly replied.

Mom continued, "Okay, Charles, since it's your money and your car, it's your decision. I love you."

I drove to town and bought a stereo. Within a month of draining my funds with this purchase, the car developed a catastrophic mechanical issue, leaving it completely undrivable. Instead of rubbing salt into the wound, my parents expressed sadness. "That's got to be so disappointing for you," they told me. My father added, "Fortunately, you have a good head on your shoulders for solving problems like this. Let me know if you want any ideas."

Their response definitely made it worse for me in the short term. Has anyone ever made it impossible for you to blame them for a problem you created? Yes, I might have gotten some grim satisfaction in the short term if my parents had been nasty toward me. What they gave me instead was an opportunity to take an honest look at my decisions and see that I alone was the architect of my misfortune.

Let Them See That You Believe in Them

When children fail to handle responsibilities well, some parents are tempted to expect less of them in the future. Both Edwin and Ava worried that there might be a repeat performance with the new mower, so they were not sure they wanted to give Max responsibility for mowing again. What if he didn't take care of it? What if he let the grass grow too long between mowings? What if he cut it too short? What if he ran over the hose? What if they had to discipline him again because he simply refused to do the chore? Wouldn't it be easier for Edwin or Ava to do the mowing themselves? I reminded them that removing responsibilities might be easier, but it would simply reward Max's irresponsibility.

The second problem with terminating responsibilities due to mistakes is that doing so sends three very discouraging messages:

- You are too slow to learn from your mistakes.
- Anything less than perfection is not acceptable.
- There is no forgiveness from me.

Third, when we take responsibilities away because our kids have blown something, we simply deprive them of the great amount of practice they need to someday become responsible teens and young adults. In fact, since they are human, our children will sometimes repeat the mistakes they have made. There's even a good chance they will make mistakes that we never anticipated. Regardless of how well we parent, such things can happen. The question is not whether our children will mess up; it's whether we are willing to take the risks required to help them become strong, confident, and virtuous adults. One such risk is allowing them to prove that they are capable of learning from our discipline and instruction.

To be clear, I am not suggesting that we should never take away *privileges*. They are certainly a different matter than responsibilities. When the potential consequences of failure could be very serious, such as life or death, it is certainly wise to take away perks at least temporarily. For example, a parent is smart to stop allowing their teen to drive if they are being reckless. The same goes for a child who is refusing to follow house rules about internet and social media use. A child who won't wear a helmet while riding their bike should not be allowed to use it until they begin following bike safety rules.

But when it came to Edwin and Ava allowing Max to resume his *responsibility* for mowing the lawn and maintaining the mower, they recognized that doing so was worth the risk. At fourteen, he knew how to use the machine safely. Now he even knew how much a mower cost and how hard it was to earn money to buy a new one. Edwin and Ava realized that they had to put aside their worry and send their son a very confident can-do message. This, they learned, is *not* communicated through more lectures or discussions about what Max needed to remember. Instead, this message was sent by simply reinstating the responsibility.

As we progress in understanding which parts of our children's spiritual growth fall within our control, and which do not, we begin to see that our beliefs and resulting style of parenting have profound implications. If we habitually try to control what's only within the power of our Creator, we end up fighting many unnecessary and hurtful power struggles. Instead, when we focus only on doing what God calls us to do, our eyes open wider in amazement and gratitude for the incomprehensible magnitude of His power, love, and faithfulness.

Realizing that our children's spiritual growth and character do not rest solely on our shoulders but are directed by God also gives us the hope and strength required to more consistently provide the love, instruction, limits, discipline, and grace our kids need. Yes, acting on these lessons requires many great leaps of faith! If we allow fear to pull us backward, causing us to try controlling what we cannot, we and our children are guaranteed to miss out on the freedom and wonderful sense of purpose that God desires for us.

Several months after our first meeting, Edwin and Ava came to my office with smiles on their faces. They proudly explained that Max had just made the junior varsity soccer team at his large high school. Even more impressive, said Edwin, was that rather than insisting he should no longer have to help in the yard, Max asked his dad if, as long as he actually did it, he could decide when over the weekend to mow. When Edwin accidently left the Weedwacker in their side yard and had to run out in a rainstorm and carry it into the garage, he laughingly groaned to Max and Ava about the perils of growing old. The foot dragging, slammed doors, and yelling matches were history.

Where to Go from Here

In part 1, we've focused on the basics: understanding the process of spiritual development; developing a truth-oriented filter; and learning how to apply the consultant style of setting limits and providing loving discipline. This enables us to model God's loving power, talk with our kids about Him, and build a relationship that fosters spiritual curiosity and personal responsibility. As we move into part 2, we will look at practices to help our kids grow in spiritual maturity. These include teaching them how to become content, generous, resourceful, and hardworking people in a temptation-laden world dominated by digital technology and social media. Finally, we will consider how to help them develop their own truth-oriented filter. A primary goal of doing all of this is to help them see that Jesus Christ is their only true source of security: "The name of the LORD is a strong fortress; the godly run to him and are safe" (Proverbs 18:10, NLT).

PART 2

MOVING TOWARD MATURITY

Helping Our Children Prepare to Launch

CHAPTER 6

SERVING, CHORES, AND ALLOWANCE

Teaching Contentment and Generosity

I sat on the edge of the platform in the church sanctuary where I'd just wrapped up the morning session of a parenting conference. While reviewing my teaching notes for the afternoon, I munched on some snacks. I looked up to see a woman carefully moving along each row of audience seats, throwing bits of paper, empty cups, and other trash into a small bucket she was carrying. Her grandson, who looked to be no older than three, followed. As she walked, this woman smiled and quietly sang, "Clean up! Clean up! Everybody clean up!"[1] Each time she spotted a piece of trash, she'd say with enthusiasm, "Look, Trevor. That's trash! That goes in the bucket."

As you might imagine, little Trevor was singing along and trying to help. Grabbing a pair of sunglasses, he exclaimed, "Look, trash!" and prepared to throw them in Grandma's bucket.

She quickly intervened, saying with great joy, "Silly! That's not trash. Those go back on the seat!"

Trevor squealed, "Silly! Not trash!"

Realizing that I was watching a real-life sermon on joy and contentment, I set aside my notes, transfixed. It was a blessing to witness. As the two moved along, they giggled and talked, with Trevor pointing at some objects and shouting, "Granny, that's silly! That's not trash!" and pointing at others, jumping up and down, and proclaiming, "Granny! Granny! That's trash. I throw it away!"

In a natural way, Grandma managed to take a mundane task and turn it into an opportunity to reflect the light of God, not only on her grandson but also on me. I'm certain that Grandma had no idea what God had done through her on that day.

We can learn from this grandma when it comes to our children's spiritual development as well. While certain aspects are solely up to God, you'll remember from chapter 1 that we do have some responsibility—to educate our children about Bible teachings and to live in ways that reflect these teachings. In all things, both large and very small, we must seek to relate to our kids in ways that paint a picture of God's strength and love. How we carry out this responsibility is just as important as the action itself.

Obviously, doing any of these tasks with a grouchy attitude will do little to get our kids excited about generously spreading the love of Jesus. As Trevor's grandma demonstrated, an attitude of excitement and joy is far more likely to make our faith attractive. Her enthusiasm rubbed off on her grandson and everyone who witnessed it. Their service that day clearly demonstrated what Christ has commanded us to do: "Let your light shine before others, so that they may see your good works and give glory to your Father who is in heaven" (Matthew 5:16).

HOW TO RAISE A CHEERFUL GIVER

As you build your own spiritual foundation on the Spirit, you can take the following steps to help your children learn the habit of sincere generosity:

- Once they can walk, have them serve by your side.
- Help them develop humility and peace rather than a sense of entitlement.
- Expect them to contribute to the family by doing chores.
- Teach them to steward money rather than be owned by it.

Once They Can Walk, Have Them Serve by Your Side

Some of my earliest, clearest, and dearest childhood memories involve visits to my great-aunt Anne's house where my parents and I would help her with light housekeeping tasks. My mom and dad would let me ring the doorbell. After what seemed an eternity, she'd open the door, smiling from ear to ear. She'd kiss me on the cheek and say, "Charlie, my lad! There you are!"

In the midst of this warm display of affection, I would smell burnt toast and strong coffee. Then she'd lead me to her kitchen where she'd prepared a table for two. On each plate was a piece of buttered toast, much of it scorched black. I washed mine down with milk as Great-Aunt Anne sipped coffee. We talked about our week, looking into each other's eyes as we did. After we ate, I helped her dust her furniture, vacuum the floor, wash the dishes, and finish other tasks. To this day, the taste of burnt toast and the smell of strong coffee leave me feeling loved and secure. So does the sound of the vacuum.

As a child, I was extremely fortunate to have many grown-ups in my life who began involving me in simple household chores and service activities when I was just old enough to walk. Because they were positive, patient, and loving, my attitude toward helping was usually a positive one.

Sadly, not everyone is so fortunate. For example, a dear friend of mine had parents who rarely allowed him to help. When he did, they constantly micromanaged and criticized him. In fact, one of his most painful memories is of the day he surprised his father by shoveling the sidewalk. Instead of being grateful, his father grumbled, "You piled the snow on the wrong side of the walk." Then his dad redid the job himself as my friend stood by and watched. After many similar experiences, my friend learned to associate helping with anxiety, sadness, and feelings of inadequacy. It took him many years to acknowledge these feelings and learn to give of his time and effort.

Other times, parents may not be gruff and critical, but they are reluctant to allow young children to help because it creates more work for them. Tasks usually take twice as much time and energy to complete when their little ones are "helping." Yet by focusing on the here and now rather than the bigger picture, parents are missing countless opportunities to build deeper relationships with their children while teaching them to see the joy that comes from contributing and giving to others.

I encourage you to create a strategic plan to include your children in helping at home. Start by making a list of all the things your children can help with. For young kids, it's important that these are small tasks they can have fun doing and feel great about. Realistically, very young children usually can't offer much real help, but it's good for them to think they can. Maybe they "help" you take the trash out by simply carrying one small item as you carry the bigger bag. Maybe they can hold a flashlight for you as you are working on the drain under the kitchen sink. Maybe they can run their toy vacuum as you run the real one. My youngest son loved doing this when he was two, often exclaiming that he was catching the spots I missed.

As your children grow older, it remains just as important to do some tasks together and to model joy and contentment. From time to time, when you see your kids working hard on a chore, ask them if you can help. Work by their side, expressing how thankful you are for the opportunity to spend time with them. Of course, do this only as long as they maintain a good level of effort and the experience is enjoyable for both of you. Parents often comment that this little strategy has caused their children, even teens, to be much more giving of their time and effort. One mother shared, "After doing this with my ten-year-old, I noticed that she started occasionally coming to me and asking if I needed her help."

Serving together outside of the home is also important. When they are young, your kids will tend to be fairly enthusiastic about it. As they get older, they may complain. When you remain firm yet loving about your expectation that they participate, your kids will usually end up feeling good about helping. I remember the first time we committed to help pack food items to be sent overseas. As we drove to the ministry warehouse, one of our sons sat stiffly in the back seat, huffing and puffing like his world was coming to an end. This irritated me, but I knew that I couldn't let him set the emotional tone for our entire family. Deciding to be happy in spite of his unhappiness, I got to work alongside my family. It wasn't long before I saw my son smiling and interacting with other people, rushing to bring more supplies to volunteers who were packing them. On our drive home, he talked almost nonstop about the experience. It was clear he enjoyed it, and more important, he had given of himself to benefit others.

Involving our children in service shows our love for them. I often find it helpful to remember that this is one of the many ways that our Father in heaven shows His love for us. From the beginning He—who needs nothing from us—invited us to play a part in His Kingdom: "The LORD God took the man and put him in the garden of Eden to work it and keep it" (Genesis 2:15).

Help Children Develop Humility and Peace Rather than a Sense of Entitlement

All of us are born with a natural bent toward self-centeredness. In families where kids are never expected to sacrifice any of their time, effort, or desires for the benefit of others, this inclination only intensifies.

I once worked with a young couple who had been persuaded that they should make children the center of attention and essentially allow them to run free. This, they were told, would make their kids happy and self-confident. As a result, these parents did everything possible to keep their little ones from getting upset. They didn't set many limits or do much in the way of discipline. When this couple came to me, they admitted how deeply frustrated they had become. Rather than being happy, their kids were becoming more and more demanding.

Ironically, by doing what they thought would lead to happiness, this mom and dad were raising selfish, unhappy, and discontented kids. Fortunately, their kids were still very young, and I worked with this couple to set some expectations that would encourage their entire family to begin honoring one another.

Adopting some basic guidelines (see "Some Suggested Expectations: Honoring God and Respecting Others" on the next page) is one of the means by which children learn to put others first. Of course, these are good guidelines, but they focus simply on behavior, not the heart. Plenty of people do good things when they know they are being watched by someone they want to impress. Their motivation for giving is transactional, based on the expectation of some type of reward. God cares about our motives, and He is not pleased or honored when we are driven by the need for recognition, pride, or material gain. This is where humility comes in: "Do nothing from selfish ambition or conceit, but in humility count others more significant than yourselves" (Philippians 2:3).

Some Suggested Expectations: Honoring God and Respecting Others

As a way to teach your children to humbly honor others, I encourage you to develop—based on your children's ages and characteristics—a list of guidelines of behavior that you expect everyone in your family to follow. One such list is below. Not all the items will apply to every family, but they will give you an idea of some expectations you may want to set for your household.

- Regularly attend church as a family.
- During mealtimes, wait to eat until the family has prayed and everyone else is ready to eat.
- Open and hold doors for others.
- Volunteer our seats when older people are standing and have no place to sit.
- Resist the impulse to rush in front of others when approaching a line.
- Eat what is served at family meals rather than complaining or demanding something different.
- Politely wait our turn to speak rather than interrupting other people.
- Put our phone or other devices down when someone is trying to speak with us.
- Clean up after ourselves.
- Pick up trash we find lying around even if we weren't the one who put it there.
- Save for the extra things we want rather than expecting to be given them.
- Maintain a pleasant attitude even when we are not the center of attention.
- Demonstrate interest in others by listening to them rather than constantly talking about ourselves.

- Attend events important to others, like weddings, birthdays, graduations, sporting events, and award ceremonies, whenever possible.
- Find ways to entertain ourselves rather than expecting others to keep us from becoming bored.

Wise parents attempt to follow the same guidelines they set for their children and then to enforce them with firmness, kindness, and grace—rather than with a legalistic attitude. Godly homes are never run like dictatorships; however, parents retain their authority while applying it in loving and reasonably flexible ways. Achieving this balance is no easy feat, but all things are possible through the grace of God.

A heart-level desire to live generously, even when it provides no personal benefit or costs us our desires or even our lives, comes only through a saving relationship with Jesus Christ. This is brought to life when the Holy Spirit living within us prompts us to recognize the overwhelming generosity of Christ's sacrifice on the cross. He gave everything so that we could be free from sin and death.

Expect Kids to Contribute to the Family by Doing Chores

One of the most important ways we can help our children develop an attitude of generosity is by teaching them the skills needed to finish chores—and then when they are around the ages of five or six, beginning to expect that they complete them without being nagged or paid. Contributing to the family in this way requires a sacrifice of time and effort. Doing chores promotes humility and shows kids that they are deeply loved and valued members of the family team. Not only does it make kids more generous, but it also helps them grow into competent, resilient, and happier adults.

> When they contribute to the family by doing chores, kids see that they are deeply loved and valued members of the family team.

In this section, I will provide a four-step plan for giving this great gift to your children. The first step involves having them help you brainstorm a list of all the things required to keep your home and family running. Yes, I'm talking about everything—including earning money, paying bills, shopping for and putting away groceries, cleaning, cooking, doing laundry, and anything else that you and your children can think of.

Patty, a single mom, decided to do this with her three boys, ages nine, seven, and five. After breakfast one Saturday, she cheerfully asked, "What do you guys think needs to be done around here to keep our family going?"

The boys seemed confused by her question. Zeke, her nine-year-old, finally responded: "I guess we have to eat, so somebody has to cook."

Patty agreed. "That's right!"

Five-year-old Sam chimed in, "Yeah, and somebody has to feed the pets."

Patty continued, "Let's make a list. I'll write, and you can help me remember all the things that need to get done."

Before long, they had a rather long list. It included feeding the dog and cat, setting the table for meals, washing and putting away the dishes, taking out the trash, dusting furniture, cleaning the floors, scrubbing the showers, cleaning the toilets, planning and preparing meals, driving the kids where they needed to go, working a job to earn money, purchasing and maintaining insurance, paying taxes and other bills, ensuring that the car was maintained, and much more. Some of the items on this list could only be completed by an adult. Others could also be done by the kids.

The second step involves creating a "Family Contributions Chart," where specific tasks are listed under each family member's name. I like the term *contributions* rather than *chores* because it has a more positive feel and communicates the basic truth that families thrive when everyone contributes.

Knowing that it would be good for her boys to see how much she does for them on a regular basis, Patty began by making a section headed "Mom's Contributions" under which she included just a few of the many things she did to keep the family running. As she did, she cheerfully said, "I feel blessed that God has made it possible for me to do these things and many others. I love to do them because I love the three of you so much!"

After finishing her section, Patty drew three other sections on the chart and wrote one of her boy's names at the top of each. Allowing them some freedom to choose, she helped them divide up the remaining responsibilities from the list they had created earlier. Each had a reasonable number of contributions listed under their name. None of these were unreasonably strenuous, time-consuming, or beyond their abilities. Next to each was a deadline for completion.

"What if we want to trade the things we want to do?" seven-year-old Tyler asked.

Patty replied, "Just ask me first. I will probably be fine with it. The main thing is that the jobs get done."

Obviously, it's important to remember that some kids need more help understanding this than others. Some will benefit from being given picture cues for each of their responsibilities. It's also wise to practice these chores with your kids if you are not completely sure they know how to do what's expected of them. As with all the skills shared in this book, you will want to approach this activity with an attitude of grace, knowing that it's okay to help your kids or adjust your expectations when necessary.

The third step involves posting your "Family Contributions Chart" and explaining that it is your children's responsibility to check it daily. As Patty taped the one they had just made onto the refrigerator, she said, "I love you guys. That's why I am no longer going to remind or nag you to do these things. Do you think that it would be smart for you to check this chart every day, just to be sure that you aren't forgetting to do anything?"

Patty's boys enthusiastically nodded and agreed to check their contributions daily. She reinforced this idea by making a big deal of doing so herself. Each day over breakfast she would think out loud in front her boys: "I better go check and see what contributions I need to make today. I don't want to forget about anything."

The fourth step involves letting your kids learn from logical consequences delivered with sincere empathy. Because the goal is to avoid reminding, lecturing, threatening, or fighting with your kids, it can be helpful to pray that they will occasionally forget or refuse to do something they are assigned. We hope and pray for such things because doing so gives us the strength to avoid giving reminders, helps us remain calmer when they do forget or refuse to cooperate, and assists us in remembering that mistakes are priceless learning opportunities.

So what might you do if one of your kids makes the mistake of forgetting or refusing to do a chore? One option is to do it for them and expect them to repay you for your time and energy. They can do so by staying home from an activity, repaying you for your time and effort by doing a more undesirable chore than the one they avoided, losing some privilege reserved only for kids who act responsibly, or experiencing some other commonsense consequence delivered with sincere empathy—not anger, frustration, or sarcasm.

One mother, tired of having to prod her defiant teenage daughter to clean her room, hired a friend of hers to do the job. When her daughter came home from school that day, she found a bill taped to her door. Yes! She did have to pay for the job. Interestingly, this improved the girl's memory quite a bit.

Let's get back to Patty and her three boys. Almost a week after they'd created the contributions chart, the boys had completed almost nothing listed on it. In the past she had constantly reminded them and even done some ranting and raving in an attempt to get them to help. Now she realized that doing so was only training them to rely on her nagging and prodding to do their chores. That, in turn, was interfering with their development of self-control and personal responsibility. This time she kept quiet and did most of their jobs herself.

Patty's kids looked forward to Saturdays, as she typically drove them across town to play with the children who lived next door to them before they had moved. This family had a pool in their backyard, and the kids loved swimming, splashing, and goofing around. Patty enjoyed the time, too, as she had developed a close relationship with the parents of these kids.

After breakfast on this Saturday, Zeke was the first to speak up. "Mom? When are we leaving?"

Sam joined in. "Yeah, Mom, we want to go swimming!"

With empathy in her voice, Patty said, "This is so sad. You didn't complete most of your contributions this week."

Tyler protested: "Yeah, but you didn't remind us!"

Patty breathed deeply and exhaled slowly. "Right," she softly agreed. "I told all of you that I wouldn't. I love you too much to nag and fight with you anymore about getting the chores done. The problem is that I spent all my time and energy this week doing the chores for you. Now I need to get some of my own work done. Besides, staying home today will give you time to catch up on anything you need to do."

"But, Mom," Zeke protested, "we won't do it again."

Tyler agreed. "Yeah, we will remember. We were really busy this week."

Sam sobbed. "But I want to swim."

Patty's heart broke as she heard the disappointment in their voices, but she knew the value of following through on her word—she had to model the behavior she wanted her sons to emulate. Teaching accountability wasn't always easy for Patty in the short term, but she knew that the payoff later would be worth it to her boys.

The benefits of allowing our children to make plenty of small, affordable mistakes like this are beyond number. By refusing to nag or yell, we avoid damaging power struggles and arguments, and we buy ourselves time to pray and remain calm. We also model God's care toward His beloved children; in His supreme strength and wisdom, He loves us too much to micromanage us. Because of this great love, He allows us to err and to face struggles in a variety of circumstances.

Before we move to another topic, I must comment on the far too common practice of consistently providing rewards or even paying kids to do their chores. Of course, there are times when it's appropriate to give our kids money for doing jobs that go far above and beyond typical family contributions. However, consistently paying or rewarding them to help is unnecessary and creates a dangerous sense of entitlement. *What do I get for being good?* is a question none of us want our children to adopt in their hearts and minds. As soon as they do, true generosity is squelched and true joy cannot be felt. An attitude of entitlement does not build spiritual strength. In contrast, notice the apostle Paul's humility as three times he credits the grace of God for all he had accomplished through great toil, suffering, and perseverance: "By the grace of God I am what I am, and his grace toward me was not in vain. On the contrary, I worked harder than any of [the apostles], though it was not I, but the grace of God that is with me" (1 Corinthians 15:10).

> By refusing to nag or yell, we avoid damaging power struggles and arguments, and we buy ourselves time to pray and remain calm. We also model God's care toward His beloved children.

Teach Children to Steward Money Rather than Be Owned by It

You don't have to look hard to find examples of people who are owned by their finances. Some have solid bank accounts and look to them for their purpose, identity, and security. Even though it seems they shouldn't have a care in the world because of their financial security, they continue to be consumed with fear that they won't have enough. Others earn plenty but spend it before they can pay all their bills. They, too, live in a constant state of uneasiness, forever fearful that they will run out of cash. In both instances, people are generally consumed with amassing more, and the thought of giving any of it away seems preposterous. They reason, *It's mine. I earned it, and I need it!*

I encourage you to seek ways to counteract this tendency early, perhaps following August's example. After a family dinner, this octogenarian smiled at Miriam, his seven-year-old great-granddaughter, and said, "I have something very important to give you, but I want you to close your eyes first."

Excited to receive his gift, Miriam held out her hand and squinted just a bit so she could watch him slowly retrieve something from his coat pocket.

"Oh, dearest Miriam, I see you peeking," August said with obvious amusement.

Miriam squeezed her eyelids together as tightly as she could. The elderly man then placed something into her hand, gently closing her fingers around it.

"What is it?" she asked excitedly. She looked down at a one-hundred-year-old silver dollar resting in the palm of her hand. On it was the profile of a woman wearing a brilliant crown.

"It's money!" Miriam cried joyfully.

Great-Grandpa August smiled and said, "Yes, but it's a lot more."

"What else is it?" she asked, puzzled.

Pointing to the coin, he replied, "It contains a priceless lesson that's far more valuable than money." He pointed to another spot on the coin and asked, "What does this say right here?"

Miriam read the words: "In God we trust."

Looking deeply into her eyes, Miriam's great-grandpa said, "I pray you will always remember to put all your trust in God, not in money or anything else. Everything we have comes from His hand. He will give us what we need, and He wants us to share it with others."

One of the greatest gifts we can give our children is the knowledge that God is our loving and trustworthy provider. When they are taught to rely on Him, not their earthly resources, they don't have to suffer from the constant anxiety, stress, and striving that comes with placing their faith in something that can be lost in an instant. The apostle Paul puts it like this: "For the love of money is a root of all kinds of evils. It is through this craving that some have wandered away from the faith and pierced themselves with many pangs" (1 Timothy 6:10).

Further, it's important to reinforce that God blesses us so that we can bless others; this way, our children have an opportunity to see that there's no need to be stingy with anything they have.

> He who supplies seed to the sower and bread for food will supply and multiply your seed for sowing and increase the harvest of your righteousness. You will be enriched in every way to be generous in every way, which through us will produce thanksgiving to God.
>
> **2 CORINTHIANS 9:10-11**

As you've surely noticed, this book is not just about teaching through talking. It's about allowing children to have real-life experiences that reinforce biblical principles. With respect to money, this can be done by providing them with a small allowance. Ideally, you would start this when they are four or five, but it's not too late if your children are older.

> One of the greatest gifts we can give our children is the knowledge that God is our loving and trustworthy provider.

Recently a couple asked me, "Charles, we like the idea of giving our children some money to practice with, but how much should it be?"

I simply replied, "Not enough."

"What do you mean?" they asked.

"Start with a very small amount," I told them. "It shouldn't be enough to buy anything. It might be fifty cents a week, a dollar, or more based on the age of your child, where you live, and a variety of other factors. You decide. The most important thing is that it's not enough for them to simply go out and buy things they want. It needs to be so little that they learn to save, to earn more, to spend wisely, and to give. Besides, you can always slowly increase the amount if you find it necessary."

One way to introduce an allowance is to simply let your children know that you want to start giving them some "practice money" once every week. They are free to do whatever they want with it, as long as they first tithe by giving 10 percent to the Lord. It's important that this tithing is done *physically* each week. The act of dropping it into the offering plate at church reinforces their awareness that they have let go of something valuable. As God works on their hearts, they will begin to see that they are simply giving back what has first come from His own hand.

It won't surprise you that I often consider the children who initially squander the money they've been given to be the most fortunate in the long term. What a lesson to be learned from experiencing these early mistakes! My prayer for your kids is the same as it was for mine when they were young: "Please, Lord, let them make plenty of small financial mistakes so that they can learn the wisdom and self-control required to avoid far more costly ones when they are older."

After listening to my suggestions on allowance, many parents ask, "This makes sense, but what do we do when our kids ask for more money? How can they earn more if we are not supposed to pay them to complete their chores?"

One simple yet effective policy you might consider is paying your kids for some tasks that fall beyond the scope of their usual family contributions. Give them this opportunity only when they are consistently responsible in completing their baseline contributions and doing quality work.

Another question that often comes up is whether it's ever appropriate to provide a loan to older kids. Some parents decide they will do so, but only if their children pay interest and provide something they value as collateral. The logic is that this will teach them about borrowing and lead them to avoid debt. Personally, I feel uneasy about this, concerned it might have the opposite effect by implying that assuming debt can be a solid financial strategy. When our kids wanted something we felt was appropriate, my wife and I would either find a way to give it to them as a gift, pay for a portion of the cost as a gift, or suggest a viable way they could earn the money to buy it.

BLESSED TO BLESS OTHERS

What does all of this have to do with helping our kids learn to be generous? When our children *experience* the fact that God really does provide for their needs, their faith strengthens. When they *truly see* that He blesses them so that they can bless others, their faith grows. When they *feel* His love and provision despite losing finances due to unforeseen circumstances or mistakes of their own, their faith matures.

Generosity is a function of faith. Faith grows incrementally each time we experience God's miraculous presence and provision in the face of what appears to be scarcity. My great-aunt didn't have an extravagant home, and she served me the simplest of breakfasts when we visited. Yet she lavished me with her love and attention, and she was one of my earliest models of what generosity and contentment look like. As our children repeatedly experience people like this, they grow in their understanding that God so abundantly provides them with time, talents, and treasure that they need not keep all these things to themselves. Completing chores and learning to steward money reinforces these lessons. Added benefits include maturation in decision-making and problem-solving abilities—critical life skills that we'll look at more closely in the next chapter.

CHAPTER 7

PRAYER, PLANNING, AND PATIENCE

Promoting Problem-Solving Skills and Resilience

Oscar had a problem. Most of the kids at school were nice, but Sean was constantly calling him names. At first it didn't bother Oscar too much, but now he was sick of it. In fact, he'd gotten so tired of hearing those names that he'd lost his temper and pushed Sean to the floor outside the cafeteria. For this, he was serving three days of in-school suspension. As he sat for his punishment, he tried to convince himself that shoving Sean had been worth it because it would make him start showing some respect. Deep down, he knew better.

Four days later, Sean proved to Oscar that knocking him on his rear hadn't solved a thing. "I hope you had a nice vacation," Sean quipped with sarcasm and a nasty sneer. "You are such a big man. Oh, Oscar—the big man! I'm soooo scared."

Livid, Oscar walked away from Sean, hiding in a bathroom stall where he quietly cried. He wasn't a bad or violent kid. He was hurting over a problem that seemed overwhelming and impossible to solve.

I met with Oscar's parents and soon realized that they were hurting and feeling a bit overwhelmed too. His father, George, added, "We don't like that he pushed that boy, but we feel horrible for our son. He's beside himself over this."

Rita, Oscar's mother, agreed. "Sean's been picking on him all year. We discussed it with the principal. She says that she's already talked to Sean about it and that there's nothing else she can do. I guess I see her point. Sean calls our son names when nobody is around to hear or see it."

As parents, problems like this break our hearts! Understandably, we want to do whatever we can to make these challenges go away. This is the right response when life and limb are in danger. When matters are not life or death, however, rescuing almost always makes things worse. Even as I listened to George and Rita, I remembered that my role was not to rescue *them*. Instead, it was to listen, empathize, help them consider a variety of possible options, and pray for them. Remember, consultants do not tend to solve problems for people but rather work to guide people toward finding their own solutions. My job was to help George and Rita learn how to do the very same things for their son. Oscar had to take primary responsibility for solving his problem with Sean. Consultant parents coach their kids to resolve their dilemmas in ways that ultimately bring glory to God.

Consultant parents coach their kids to resolve their dilemmas in ways that ultimately bring glory to God.

THE TRUTH ABOUT PROBLEMS AND THEIR SOLUTIONS

Helping our children develop problem-solving skills and resilience is far easier and more effective when we do the following:

- Remember that we don't have to face life's challenges alone.
- Pause to pray before acting.

- Guide our kids to own and solve their problems.
- Start as early in their lives as possible.
- Remember that it is never too late to start.

Remember That We Don't Have to Face Life's Challenges Alone

The simple truth about problems is this: We are guaranteed to face them. The Bible makes this clear, but it also emphasizes that God will see us through. We don't have to face them alone.

> Many are the afflictions of the righteous,
> but the LORD delivers him out of them all.
>
> **PSALM 34:19**

We see this same pattern in a later psalm:

> Cast your burden on the LORD,
> and he will sustain you;
> he will never permit
> the righteous to be moved.
>
> **PSALM 55:22**

We read yet another example in the Gospel of John:

> [Jesus says,] "In this world you will have trouble. But take heart! I have overcome the world."
>
> **JOHN 16:33, NIV**

This "problem-provision" pattern is repetitively threaded into the tapestry of Scripture. We see it in the small problems and the large, the heaviest of which is our sin. Through our own efforts, this problem is too great to overcome. The harder our pride leads us to work, the more we slip. As we continue to fall, it is clear that the chasm is too steep and wide for us to climb from through our own effort. In contrast, when we humble ourselves before God and express our faith in His provision, He lifts us up. Because of Christ's work on the cross, we are cleansed and free to enter into relationship with Him: "All have sinned and fall short of the glory of God, and are justified by his grace as a gift, through the redemption that is in Christ Jesus" (Romans 3:23-24). To be completely clear, this does not mean that we will always be comfortable, prosperous, healthy, and carefree just because we trust Christ. What it does mean is that because our eternity with Him is secure, we can experience hope even in tough circumstances. It also means that He will use the challenges we face to bring glory to Himself.

It is good to teach our kids that problems are a predictable part of life in this fallen and unpredictable world. Peace comes from relying on God to carry us through these times. Hope is the product of seeing God's provision as we face our problems; in contrast, fear and discouragement reign when we don't depend on Him. A friend of mine who employed many young adults in his business told me that he has noticed one consistent difference between his most successful and least successful employees: their attitude toward problems. He's convinced that much of that has to do with how they were parented as kids. Some seem used to facing and solving challenges, while others seem to have almost no experience with this.

He particularly remembers two employees whom he'd hired for the customer service team at about the same time. Less than six months into the job, one was overwhelmed and hopeless. He told my friend: "I'd be happy here, but it's like there's always some sort of problem. Every day there's one problem after another. If there weren't so many problems, everything would be fine."

The other employee was also very young but had a completely different attitude. After a particularly difficult day, my friend thanked him for remaining cheerful while solving so many problems. This young man's response was telling: "You are welcome. I'm actually thankful for all these problems. If we didn't have any around here, I wouldn't have this job."

Would George and Rita be like the parents of the young employee who struggled or the one who confidently resolved customer complaints? They realized that, when it came to Sean's bullying, taking matters into their own hands might relieve Oscar in the short run but would also make him question his own agency. Children who grow up facing manageable problems tend to be far happier and more secure teens and young adults. In a systematic review of thirty-eight studies, researchers observed "a direct relationship between helicopter parenting and symptoms of anxiety and depression."[1] Findings like this simply confirm what God's Word teaches. There is divine purpose in struggle: *Hope is found not by avoiding problems but by experiencing God's purpose for them.*

Hope is found not by avoiding problems but by experiencing God's purpose for them.

Pause to Pray Before Acting

When facing problems, one of the greatest temptations is to leap forward before carefully considering the path we will take. The bigger the problem, the more tempted we are to skip over seeking wisdom in prayer. Oscar's parents were struggling with this. Even though they saw the value of teaching Oscar to solve this problem, their anger made them want to lash out. George admitted, "There's a big part of me that wants to go nuclear with the school district. I want to get a lawyer and sue them."

Rita patted him on the back and said to him lovingly, "Both of us go back and forth on that. I think we both know that's not a good plan, but we still think about it."

George smiled at his wife and then looked my way. "Yeah. We are all messed up over this."

Knowing that we all needed direction, I asked, "Is it okay if we pray over this now, or is there something you'd like to share with me before we do?"

George and Rita looked at each other and turned toward me. George said, "I think we are ready. Yeah. We can go ahead and pray."

"Dear Lord," I prayed, "we are so thankful for how You love us, comfort us, and guide us through the tough times we face. You tell us that we ought to be thankful when we face trials because they help us grow. Lord, this is a hard thing to do. How can we be grateful in this situation? Oscar is hurting, and so are his parents. Please comfort them, guide them, and show them what You want them to learn from this trial. We seek Your wisdom, knowing without any doubt that You will provide it."

George continued, "Yes, Jesus, please help us. We've tried to figure this out, but we are just making ourselves crazy. Thanks, Jesus. Amen."

After pausing to take a deep breath, Rita shared, "Your prayer for us made me think about a sermon we heard. It was about looking for what God wants us to learn from the bad stuff we face. I hadn't thought about it until now, but maybe there is something that God wants us to learn from all of this."

George nodded. "God wants Oscar to learn how to handle stuff like this without getting so upset. I think He wants him to learn how to be strong."

"Yes, if we try to make all of this just go away ourselves," Rita said, "I'm worried Oscar will come to believe that he is weak and lacks independence."

"But what do we do?" George asked anxiously. "When I was a kid, I admit we just solved it with fists—kind of like what Oscar did when he knocked Sean down. I know that won't work, but I'm out of ideas. We already told the school about it. They can't seem to do anything more. We told Oscar to ignore the kid and stay away from him. That failed too."

"I can share some ideas if you are interested," I said. "As I do, I'd like to teach you some steps for helping kids own and solve their problems. Are you interested?"

Both George and Rita smiled and nodded their heads. They were ready.

Guide Our Kids to Own and Solve Their Problems

This chapter is not only about helping children handle the problem of bullying. It's about helping them learn how to approach every problem they will encounter throughout their lives. Each problem is unique, but the same process applies for solving each one. It starts with seeking wisdom far greater than any book, internet search, podcast, or other man-made resource can provide. As I did with George and Rita, we must first pause and pray.

We know that faith without works is dead (see James 2:14-17). Wisdom gained through prayer that is not acted upon is also worthless. Because God is a perfect parent, He expects us to do some work! He's not going to do everything for us because that would not be good for us. Here are five concrete steps you can take:

Step 1: Empathize, listen, and pray with your kids. Offering empathy and actively listening aren't just acts of compassion. Doing this enables us to

- reduce the odds of rebellion,
- avoid becoming the target of blame if things go poorly,
- teach responsibility, and
- take good care of ourselves.

Unfortunately, empathy is too frequently confused with sympathy. Let's take a closer look at what it truly means to empathize versus sympathize. *Sympathy* is "an affinity, association, or relationship between persons or things such that whatever affects one affects the other similarly."[2] This definition emphasizes that when we sympathize, we are affected *similarly* as the person who is facing the problem. In contrast, a good definition of *empathy* is: "the action of understanding, being aware of, being sensitive to, and vicariously experiencing the feelings, thoughts, and experience of another."[3] From this definition, we see that empathizing with someone involves being *aware of and sensitive to* their struggles and emotions. It doesn't mean adopting them.

A key word in this definition of empathy is "vicariously." It means imagining another's experience, not owning it. We are aware and demonstrate care, but do not take responsibility for a problem that is not our own. With this boundary in place, we can provide compassion while still allowing others to experience the grace and power of God as they struggle through the trials they are facing.

True empathy is difficult to grasp, particularly when the person involved is our child. More often, sympathy is our first response: "whatever affects one affects the other similarly." After all, when someone we love hurts, we hurt right along with them. Not only that, but it's normal and healthy to want to see an end to our child's pain.

We must, however, make the shift into empathy, realizing that we do others no good if we are just as overwhelmed, anxious, angry, or discouraged as they are. Expressing empathy also prevents the development of unhealthy dependency and the resulting resentment. With empathy, we are keeping ourselves out of the spotlight: We are not seen as the hero when things go well or the villain when they don't.

Along with being empathetic, we can remember that God is sovereign and perfectly loving. This knowledge of His sovereignty helps us avoid trying to control the situation in unhealthy ways.

A sixteen-year-old girl once told me how controlled she felt by her extremely sympathetic mother: "I don't feel like I can tell my mom anything because it's like she always gets more upset about it than I am. Then she tries to fix everything. We always get in a big fight, because I never asked her to fix it. I just wanted to tell her about it. Then she is hurt because she doesn't think I'm thankful for her help. It's exhausting! One of my friends has an emotional support dog. Sometimes I kind of feel like I'm my mom's emotional support human."

After I described the difference between empathy and sympathy, George and Rita made a discovery. In the past, they had spent too much time feeling sorry for Oscar, more or less communicating that it was their job to fix things. Both found it helpful when I described how another mother overcame this habit, replacing sympathy with empathy.

Eleven-year-old Jeremy had developed the bad habit of taking his coat off during recess or on the bus and forgetting it. He'd lost two coats that way in the past year. Now it had happened again. As you read each of the dialogues below, consider for yourself which response by Kathy, Jeremy's mom, is more likely to help him develop confidence and strong character. Here is her old way of responding to her son losing his coat:

Mom: Where's your coat? I saw you leave for school this morning with it on.
Jeremy: I set in on the bench at recess, but it was gone when I went to get it!
Mom: That's terrible! Did you talk to your teacher about it?
Jeremy: Yeah, but she said that I had to check the lost and found after class.
Mom: She didn't help you find it? That is really upsetting. I am so mad.
Jeremy: Yeah, and she didn't even care.

Mom: I'm so sorry that happened. It's cold. Were you cold on the bus?
Jeremy: Uh, it was kinda cold. Well, yeah, I was really cold. It was freezing. I was shivering.
Mom: I bet. I'm so upset by this! Now your dad and I have to buy you another. This is so frustrating! Why can't you be more responsible?
Jeremy: Why are you blaming me? It wasn't my fault!
Mom: Don't talk to me like that. I'm only trying to help.
Jeremy: How do you think I feel?
Mom: I am just so mad. This is the last time I am buying you a new one!
Jeremy: Well, this makes me mad too. I want one without a hood this time. I don't like ones with hoods, especially like the one that just got stolen. That fur around the hood looked so weird.

Now consider this mom's new way of responding to her son losing his coat with empathy instead of sympathy:

Mom: Where's your coat? I saw you leave for school this morning with it on.
Jeremy: I set in on the bench at recess, but it was gone when I went to get it!
Mom: I bet you were really upset when you couldn't find it.
Jeremy: Yeah, and my teacher wouldn't let me look for it in the lost and found until after school.
Mom: She said that you had to wait?
Jeremy: Yeah. She wouldn't let me go until after class. She doesn't even care!
Mom: I can see that you are really upset about this.
Jeremy: Well, aren't you?

Mom: I feel really bad for you. I can imagine that this has got to be kind of scary for you.
Jeremy: Uh, scary? What?
Mom: Well, I'm guessing that you are probably wondering where it is and what you are going to do. Would you like a hug?
Jeremy: I guess.
Mom: I'm feeling for you. The best way to solve any problem is to first ask God for His help. He loves you. Why don't we pray about this?

Mom's old way created drama and made the problem her own. Her new way expressed concern and compassion, but kept the focus on her child's feelings, which opened the door for him to own the solution. This approach helps kids develop confidence and responsibility rather than a sense of victimhood.

An important note before we move to the second step: This process for guiding kids to own and solve their problems should be reserved for situations that are not crises requiring immediate action. In those urgent cases, parents are wise to be very directive, giving themselves permission to temporarily operate like helicopters, drill sergeants, or both. Even so, one of the most critical life skills we can pass on to our kids is the ability to navigate and solve problems, and the following steps are appropriate in most nonemergency situations.

Step 2: Gently yet firmly hand the problem back. The next step in the problem-solving process involves asking the following question: "What do you think you are going to do about this?"

This question sends two very healthy underlying messages. The first is "This is your problem to solve." The second is "I believe you are capable." Both of these messages are very loving but may create some short-term anxiety for our children. Such discomfort almost always causes them to react by asking, "Well, what am I supposed to do?"

This is actually a beautiful question. God is pleased when we humble ourselves by asking this question of Him. Likewise, we ought to be overjoyed when we hear it from our kids, and it leads us right into the next step.

Step 3: Ask, "Would you like to hear what some kids [or other people] decide to do?" When others ask for help, it's tempting to immediately share advice. Through many years of experience, I have learned that asking this question shows kids respect and sends the message that we think they are capable. Immediately offering suggestions is rarely as effective as first getting them to make a firm commitment that they truly want to hear them. This agreement is confirmed when they respond to the question "Would you like to hear what some people decide to do?" with a very clear yes. It's even better if they do so while looking squarely into your eyes and nodding their head.

Let's consider an example of a parent seeking this commitment from a child who appears rather ambivalent about wanting their help:

Child: What am I supposed to do?
Parent: Would you like to hear what some kids decide to do?

The child looks down and shrugs her shoulders.

Parent: It doesn't look like you are very interested in hearing ideas.
Child: I guess I am.
Parent: Honey, I'm happy to give ideas for solving your problem, but I need to see that you really want them. I will

> know this when you look into my eyes and tell me that you do.

Parents often ask, "What if my kid doesn't seem to want my ideas? What do I do if they flat out tell me that they don't? What if they tell me that they want my ideas but choose not to solve their problem?"

For problems that are not crises but create hardship for others as long as they remain unsolved, we may eventually need to solve the problem for our child, reserving the right to provide reasonable consequences. A parent shared this example:

> Our six-year-old son had too many toys and was leaving many of them scattered around the living room. One Saturday morning, we asked him whether he wanted some ideas on how he might solve the problem. When he agreed, we gave him some ideas and a deadline to get the problem solved before he went to bed on Sunday night. He didn't lift a finger to solve the problem, so we waited until he was at school and placed everything he didn't put away in our attic above the garage. That afternoon, we were empathetic but firm, "Jake, this is so sad. You didn't solve the problem with your toys, so we did. The toys you pick up you get to keep. The ones you don't we get to keep."
>
> He was extremely upset about this, but he's learned to do a better job of picking things up. He also takes it a lot more seriously when we let him know that he has a problem that he has to solve.

One of the greatest lessons a young person can learn is that ignoring problems always creates greater hardship than solving them. The earlier they learn this important life lesson, the happier and more productive their lives will be.

Step 4: Provide a menu of options and help them evaluate each. When your kids do demonstrate that they would like ideas for solving a problem, provide two or three options, using this format:

> Some kids [or people] decide to ________________________ _________. How will that work for you?

Using this precise language is very important. First, the aspect of choice needs to be preserved. "Some kids decide to" does this. Saying "You should" does not offer an option and will often lead to an unwinnable argument or power struggle.

Second, including the question "How will that work for you?" prompts our children to consider the consequences of each suggestion we offer. Children need as much practice with cause-and-effect thinking as possible. In Scripture, we see the importance of first counting the costs associated with any decision: "For which of you, desiring to build a tower, does not first sit down and count the cost, whether he has enough to complete it?" (Luke 14:28).

When offering ideas to our children, it can often be helpful to provide a not-so-great option first. Introducing a mediocre or even downright lousy strategy as a first option often catches children's attention and encourages them to start thinking about the consequences. It also provides an opportunity for them to experience a sense of autonomy by saying something like, "That's a horrible idea." One parent put it well: "Kids tend to reject the first option you give them, so don't waste a good one by sharing it first."

Step 5: Allow them to choose the solution. Because we love our kids, it's easy for us to make the mistake of directing them toward one solution over another. I've also had wise parents ask me, "What do I do if my child likes the bad solution I've offered, or if they come up with something else that will surely work out poorly?" Of course, we always retain the right to say no if our kids propose an option that will have a terrible outcome. Even so, it's important to remember that failure can be an incredibly effective teacher. If things do go poorly for them, it's important that we express empathy while allowing the consequences to do the teaching.

We as parents should not be surprised or allow ourselves to remain discouraged when our children choose to learn the hard way. Many great and godly people have had to learn in this fashion. In the parable of the prodigal son (see Luke 15:11-32), we meet a young man with a problem. He was unhappy with life on his dad's estate. His solution was to ask his father for his share of the inheritance so he could live someplace more fun and exciting. Instead of withholding it, his father gave him what he asked for, effectively allowing him to make an extremely poor decision. The son wasted the money on wild living, ending up starving and desperate. Coming to his senses, he decided to repent of his sin and ask forgiveness from his father. While still far off, his father spotted him, ran to meet him, and greeted him with a kiss. He also gave him a robe, placed a ring on his finger, gave him shoes for his feet, and proclaimed with great joy, "My son was dead, and is alive again; he was lost, and is found" (verse 24).

Failure can be an incredibly effective teacher, but it's important that we express empathy while allowing the consequences to do the teaching.

The lessons in this parable are many, but I'd like to highlight three ways that the father blessed his rebellious son. First, he gave him the freedom to pursue a very unwise course of action. Second, he blessed his son by allowing him to experience the consequences. Third, when his son demonstrated true remorse, the father showered him with unimaginable grace as he not only forgave his son but also lavished good things upon him.

Our ultimate goal is to help our children see that God is always by their side. We do so when we help them prayerfully consider each solution. We do so when we encourage them to seek Him when the solutions they chose don't go as they wished. We also do so when we express praise and thankfulness to God when things do go well. We are wise to do these things when our kids face struggles. Of course, they also need to witness us following similar steps when *we* encounter problems.

One of the most important things we must teach our children is that God is the unchanging source of all good things: "Every good gift and every perfect gift is from above, coming down from the Father of lights, with whom there is no variation or shadow due to change" (James 1:17). God is the sovereign Creator and sustainer of the universe, and He does not change like the phases of the moon. Therefore, we can always rely on Him to meet our needs. Are your children developing the habit of praising Him for every good thing they experience?

George and Rita followed these steps as they coached their son, Oscar, to solve his problem with Sean. First, they simply sat with him after another tough day at school, recognizing that Oscar needed to experience their empathetic presence before they helped him explore the nuts and bolts of how he might solve his problem with the bully.

"We want you to know that we love you, Son," George began. "I know that this is hard."

"I'm fine," Oscar replied, looking at the floor.

"I know that you are going to be okay," Rita added, "but this thing with Sean has got to be so frustrating."

"Yeah, whatever," Oscar answered. "He's just such a—well, whatever. It's fine."

As George and Rita continued to listen, Oscar began to open up about his feelings of frustration. As tears began to stream down his face, they prayed together, asking God for His help. They also prayed for Sean, knowing that God wants us to do this for those who oppose us.

After praying, George asked his son, "Oscar, what do you think you are going to do about this?"

Oscar was surprised. "How am I supposed to know? Nothing works."

George continued, "Would you like to hear what some kids decide to do when stuff like this happens?"

"What?" Oscar replied.

"Some kids decide to just keep doing what they are already doing. How will that work for you?" George inquired.

"That won't work," Oscar complained.

"I think you are right," George agreed. "Would you like another idea?"

"I guess so. Yeah," Oscar said.

"Some kids decide they are going to joke with the kid when they say something sarcastic or rude. How will that work for you?"

Oscar seemed confused. "What do you mean?"

George explained, "If the kid calls them a name, they experiment with acting like they aren't bothered by it. They even smile and say something like, 'Thanks for letting me know about that.'"

Oscar smiled. "That's weird, Dad."

"Yeah, I guess," George agreed.

Rita chimed in, "We've been learning that bullies are less likely to tease someone who doesn't appear upset about what they say or do. The less upset we seem to be, the less power they have."

Cautiously optimistic, Oscar answered, "I guess that might work. I don't know."

George continued, "Another thing that some kids decide to do is to slowly walk away and stand where an adult can see and hear them. They don't look at the adult or say anything to them. They just stand there. How will that work for you?"

"I don't know," Oscar admitted. "I guess I could try it."

George answered, "I'm not sure either, but I know that God will help you. If any kid can do this, you can."

Rita agreed, "It might take some experimenting, but God has given you a great mind. We believe in you."

Clearly thinking hard about all of this, Oscar added, "Yeah, but I think I should tell the principal when Sean is picking on me at lunch. She should make him sit at another table."

Rita smiled. "That's something else you can consider doing. It's always smart to ask God for help. Why don't we pray that God would show you what to do?"

As the days passed, Oscar began trying to apply some of these ideas. He struggled with Sean, he struggled with his own emotions, and he struggled with God. Sean's behavior got worse as he tried harder and harder to get Oscar to retaliate. Whenever Oscar was tempted to lash out, he silently prayed a Scripture his grandmother had shared with him when he told her about Sean: "Do not be overcome by evil, but overcome evil with good" (Romans 12:21).

Remembering this Scripture didn't seem to improve Sean's behavior, but it did help Oscar cope with it. This caught the attention of Oscar's teacher and the principal. As they noticed him trying so hard, they ramped up their efforts to keep an eye on the situation. When they did, they began to discover how sneaky and mean Sean was acting. This led them to assign him a different table at lunch and pull him from the playground as soon as he began to misbehave. Oscar's situation began to improve as Sean discovered that picking on him was no longer paying off.

Oscar shared his good fortune with his parents. "Grandma and I worked it out."

George and Rita were perfectly fine with not receiving any credit for this success. Rita replied, "I'm happy for you! God is good! He gave you an amazing grandma!"

George added, "God doesn't always keep bad stuff from happening, but He helps us get through the bad stuff."

Q & A: What Might You Do When Your Kids Engage in Sibling Rivalry?

Helping our kids navigate bullying and mistreatment outside the home is a challenge—but it is also painful when we see our own children fighting or being unkind to one another. Sibling rivalry, however, is a problem many families face. Few things are more frustrating and even heartbreaking than seeing our kids constantly pick at each other. Parents often ache over feeling as if their dream of a happy, loving family has been lost. The good news is the same truth that gives us hope in all trials: God is love, and God is firmly in control. He is more than able to use the conflict that may be present in our children's relationships with each other to help them learn to face and resolve relationship problems. We can participate in this process when we remember some important principles:

- **In most ongoing conflicts, both parties play a role.** This is why it's important to avoid taking sides or trying to find out who "started it." Very often, one child quietly jabs away with nasty looks and nasty actions done out of sight of the parents. When the child who suddenly erupts is the only one to receive discipline, this inadvertently rewards the hurtful, sneaky behavior of the other.

  Of course, there are also occasions when it is crystal clear that one child is driving the problem. In such cases, it's wise to discipline this child. It's also smart to help the other child learn skills for responding to bullies.

- **Children grow when they are expected to work out their differences.** God does not make everything easy for us, and we should not make everything easy for our kids. Doing so deprives them of the need to develop skills and most tragically the blessing of knowing their desperate need for Christ. Applying the same five-step framework covered on pages 143–154, we can provide empathy and accountability while helping our children exercise their solution-finding skills.

  There are times when it's wise to simply provide consequences rather than going through the process of guiding our children to think through solutions. Of course, there are plenty of times when it's best to do both! The overall goal is to help our kids learn how to think. When parents always rely on consequences or punishment to do the teaching, kids don't get practice owning and solving the messes they've created. This reminds me of how a child I once knew complained about his parents using Love and Logic. With great sincerity, he lamented, "I'd rather get yelled at and spanked! Now my parents are always saying stuff like, 'How are you going to solve this problem?'"

- **Kids need to be held accountable for how their behavior affects the entire family.** When our kids bicker and fight, it doesn't just affect them. It harms the rest of the family. Because of this, it's very important that they be expected to make restitution by doing things that improve the quality of life of everyone involved. This may involve doing extra chores, staying home with a kind but extremely boring babysitter so that their parents can go on a relaxing date, or staying home so their parents can rest instead of having to drive them to the places they want to go. Personally, I have a very clear memory of missing one of my youth baseball games because my dear mother needed some time to rest after having to deal with me hassling my sisters. In true Love and Logic form, she delivered the news with empathy and kindly allowed me to learn from the consequences rather than resorting to anger, lectures, or sarcasm.

Sibling spats are not always an indication of unhealthy parenting or family dynamics. Instead, they are often a normal part of growing up. When we as parents guide our children toward resolving their conflicts, hold them accountable for how these conflicts affect others, and keep a watchful eye on how we might be falling into some less-than-healthy patterns, the odds are high that God will use these struggles to help everyone learn some very important lessons.

Start as Early in Their Lives as Possible

My wife and I received a surprise blessing in middle age: a baby boy! Our older boys were already young adults, so we were both very excited and quite humbled. About the time our young son began to walk and talk, Gloria, a teacher friend of ours, asked if we were already using Love and Logic with him. "I love the five steps for guiding kids to own and solve their problems," she told us. "That's something parents should start teaching as early in their children's lives as possible."

As parents of a toddler, we couldn't imagine using this skill quite yet. He had just started to speak a few small words. How could he possibly learn this strategy?

Expressing this attitude to my friend, I tried to be gracious. "Well, he's only thirteen months old. I'm not sure how that will work."

Gloria laughed and replied, "Are you sure?"

Because she was a specialist in early childhood education, I wanted to hear more. "What do you mean?"

"This is a great time to start modeling it," she continued. "Whenever you face any sort of problem or decision, let him overhear you thinking it through. Let's say that you are having trouble buckling his car seat. Let him hear you tell yourself, 'This thing isn't working. This is a problem. Problems can be hard, but you can learn a lot from them. I wonder what I should do. Let's see. Some people decide to turn the strap around and try it this way. I wonder how this will work for me. Oh, that's too bad. That didn't work. Other people decide to push it in at this angle. I wonder how that will work. Look at that! It worked. God is good! He helped me solve that problem.'"

My wife smiled and said, "That makes total sense! He copies just about everything we do. If he can learn our bad habits, he can learn the good ones too."

Gloria's advice led us to model this process as often as possible, doing our best to make it part of our daily lifestyle. When our son was about three, he observed Monica struggling with her computer. Approaching her, he said, "So sad, Mommy. What are you going to do?"

Surprised, she asked, "What?"

He didn't miss a beat. "Computer is broke. Do you want ideas?"

Of course, she was open to his suggestions. "Sure, honey. What do some people decide to do?"

Smiling from ear to ear, he said, "Some people run it over with their trike. How will that work?"

Before she could reply, he laughed and ran off to play for a bit. Circling back, he stopped briefly to share another idea. "Some people turn it off and on." Then he ran off again.

Taking his advice, Monica rebooted the laptop, seeing immediately that the problem had resolved itself.

Our youngest son is now a college student studying mechanical engineering. Recently, he was asked by a relative why he was so passionate about this field. Predictably, he answered, "I love making things. To do that you have to solve a lot of problems. It's so cool to see how math and science and technology work together to do that. It's crazy hard, but it is great."

One of the greatest gifts we can give our children is to allow them to see us encountering problems. If we start early by modeling the thoughts and actions required to solve them, the odds go up that they will be far more successful. When they see us relying on God and giving Him the glory, they will be far more likely to develop this habit as well. What our children learn early in their lives—often before they seem capable of understanding much of anything—will have a dramatic and lasting impact on their lifelong path. That's one reason to begin reading the Bible to your children while they are still in the womb.

Remember That It Is Never Too Late to Start

I've heard the following from many very tired and stressed parents: "How does this apply to my kids? They're adults for crying out loud. Is it too late?"

As long as there is breath in their lungs, there is hope for change. In fact, 100 percent of the principles included in this book, as well as about 99 percent of the specific strategies, also apply to adults. This is great news, given the fact that a huge proportion of parents express deep concern over their relationships with their adult children, as well as the quality of decisions these children are making.

A very common scenario involves young or middle-aged adult kids who are not particularly warm with their parents yet repetitively depend on them to bail them out. Eric was a classic example. Instead of overcoming his lack of responsibility with age, he always picked up the phone and dumped it on his father. Rather than being thankful and making consistent efforts to mature, he felt entitled to be rescued. It was an ugly dance that had been going on for decades between him and his father, Mike.

Things finally began to change when Eric traded in his Jeep for a used Harley-Davidson. This created three problems: First, people with a history of making rash decisions are probably the last who should operate a vehicle with a powerful engine and only two wheels. Second, he lived in Colorado where it snows a lot in the winter. Third, this "deal" left him completely strapped for cash.

By the middle of October, Eric was beginning to wonder if he'd made such a great decision. By November, snow began to fly, and he was sure that he hadn't. Picking up the phone, he dialed his father. After getting through the obligatory niceties, Eric got to the point: "I was just wondering if you could give me a quick loan. I'm a little short on cash, and I need to pick up something I can drive to work."

In their relationship, "Can you give me a quick loan?" really meant

"I demand that you give me money." Mike had grown up in a family where generosity was regarded as a top value, so he was the sort who'd give someone the shirt off his back. Unfortunately, Eric had abused his father's kindness, causing his father to dip way too deeply into his shallow retirement savings. The last time this happened, Mike talked it over with a pastor at his church. This very godly man offered his prayers and some wisdom: "You are full of grace toward others. That's an admirable thing, but I wonder whether giving Eric money every time he demands it is actually hurting him. If you are interested, I can share some ideas. They might be hard for you to do, but they will help Eric in the long term."

Highly motivated to help his son, Mike accepted this offer, listening carefully as the pastor taught him the five steps for guiding kids to own and solve their problems. Knowing that it wouldn't be long before Eric asked to be rescued again, Mike set his mind on getting prepared to use the steps. So this time, when Eric asked for another "loan" to buy a car, Mike responded differently.

With empathy instead of sympathy he replied, "It sounds like you are in a jam. That's rough. What's going on?"

"This winter the county isn't plowing at all," Eric complained. "The streets are always a mess. The road crews aren't getting to anything. Last winter wasn't so bad."

Resisting the temptation to argue about his son's attempt to deflect responsibility, Mike continued to empathize. "That sounds difficult."

A bit irritated, Eric steered the conversation back to the topic of money. "I need to get a car. Can you give me a loan?"

"I'd love to, Son," Mike replied gently yet firmly, "but you haven't repaid me for the last one I gave you."

"But I'm good for it," Eric answered, obviously surprised by the boundary his dad was setting.

Mike was at a temporary loss for words.

"Are you still there? Dad?"

"Yes, I'm here. What do you think you are going to do to solve this problem?"

"I don't know why you are making this such a big deal," Eric said, his voice rising.

Continuing the process he'd learned, Mike asked, "Would you like to hear what some people decide to do in this sort of situation?"

Eric was too angry to listen. "I thought you were a Christian. You're just selfish! Never mind!"

Mike was ready for this. He knew that things might go very poorly, but he was determined to end the pattern of rescuing. His son's future depended on it. As such, the ultimate act of grace was to say no and to allow his son to truly own the problem he faced. "I'm happy to share some ideas with you, but I can't loan you any money," Mike said.

Eric hung up.

Tears sprang to Mike's eyes as he let out a deep sigh, but he was comforted by the fact that he had not reacted by arguing, yelling, or doing anything else that was hurtful. He'd stood his ground, even though it felt like it was crumbling beneath him.

As time went by, Mike continued to reach out to his son, offering love. Each time, the conversation was tense, often ending with Mike having to calmly yet firmly say no to a request for money.

When Mike called a few weeks before Christmas, Eric quipped sarcastically, "Thanks for nothing! Now I have to ride the bus most days. Have you seen some of the people who ride the bus? I still can't believe how selfish you are. God says that you are supposed to take care of family when they have needs."

Mike was tempted to reply with "Eric, *you* are the people who ride the bus! Besides, the Bible also says that you reap what you sow." Fortunately, he didn't. God helped him hold his tongue. Instead, he answered, "I know this is hard for you, but I thank God that you have an option that will keep you a lot safer than trying to ride that bike on ice and snow. I love you and am always praying for you."

Mike had discovered that he needed to walk a different path with his son, the only one leading to hope. When we go out of our comfort zones by doing so, we are like the nation of Israel as they stepped out of Egypt toward the Promised Land. Every journey toward something better requires great struggle, discomfort, and risk. We can either turn back in defeat or press forward in faith. God will allow tests to occur, but He will also give us the means for passing through them. As I've heard it said, "If He can part the sea, He will provide for thee."

THE CASE OF THE MISSING COAT

Earlier in this chapter I shared two examples. Both involved a child who had lost his coat at school, claiming it had been "stolen." One showed how Kathy's use of sympathy led her to own the problem, leaving her son feeling more anxious and helpless. The other demonstrated how this mom learned to use empathy to help her son take ownership of the problem. This new way was scary because it required that she relinquish some control. As you will see, this led to her son receiving a priceless gift.

After empathizing, listening, and praying with her son, Jeremy, Kathy asked, "What do you think you are going to do?"

"I don't know. Besides, I told you that somebody probably stole it. What am I supposed to do about that?" he replied.

Kathy answered calmly, "I don't know, but I can share what some kids decide to do. Are you interested?"

Jeremy looked her way and nodded. "Yeah, sure."

"I guess that some kids decide to layer a lot of shirts or sweaters. How will that work for you?" she asked.

Eyes wide, Jeremy answered, "That's a terrible idea. This is Michigan!"

"Yes, that's probably not a great idea," Kathy agreed. "Some kids decide to buy a new one with the money they have saved. How will that work for you?"

Jeremy's eyes got even wider. "No way. Coats are expensive!"

"I only have one other idea," Kathy said. "Some kids decide to ask their mom to take them to a resale shop so they can find an older one they can afford. How will that work for you?"

Jeremy was upset. "Aw, Mom! Why do I have to buy a used coat when this wasn't even my fault?"

Kathy didn't bring up Jeremy's habit of losing coats, only to claim they'd been stolen. She simply replied, "I know this is hard, but I also know that God will help you solve this problem. Would you like to pray?"

Jeremy declined her offer, running to his room. A few minutes later, he emerged with his wallet, sheepishly asking her to drive him to a thrift shop. Looking through the racks of used clothing, he found a rather well-worn but stylish coat. "This one is awesome, Mom, and it's only fifteen bucks!" he proclaimed excitedly, temporarily forgetting that he was supposed to be sullen and mad.

Jeremy continued to be proud of his purchase, often telling others he'd found the coat himself and even paid for it with his own money. His mother noticed that he was also extremely protective of it, making sure to write his name clearly on the tag. Sharing her experience in one of my parenting workshops, she marveled, "It's amazing. He was so proud of the fact that he solved that problem! Finding and buying that old worn-out coat was a far more meaningful gift than anything we'd ever given him."

Is there any greater gift than knowing that God provides what we need to face every problem we encounter?

CHAPTER 8

GIVING THEM MOXIE AND MOTIVATION

Helping Kids Succeed in School and Life

Jim and Shirley's ten-year-old son spent most of every school day taking trips: trips to the pencil sharpener, trips to time-out, trips to the principal's office, and trips in his own mind to remote planets where school had yet to be invented. Learning was hard for him, so from the first week of kindergarten, he had seemed irresistibly drawn toward any activity or place that didn't require it. Of course, Jim and Shirley were deeply concerned about their boy. The questions *How can we help him love learning?* and *What's going to happen to him if he doesn't start doing better in school?* constantly ran through their minds.

Jim and Shirley were good people who loved their son deeply. Their two older daughters excelled in school, so they were convinced that if they just tried hard enough, they could help their son do better. They conscientiously helped him with his homework, arranged for tutoring, had him evaluated by educational specialists, and did their best to keep tabs on what was going on each week at school so they could support him. Instead of helping, though, his grades did not improve. Jim and Shirley were discouraged: They seemed to spend more time getting into power struggles with their boy than enjoying the son God had so graciously given them.

As Christian parents, they wanted their son to do well in school *and* become the man God created him to be. They knew that God gives each of us different gifts and that He cares far less about how lofty our achievements are than how faithfully we live out our gifts and display His love: "Whatever you do, work heartily, as for the Lord and not for men, knowing that from the Lord you will receive the inheritance as your reward. You are serving the Lord Christ" (Colossians 3:23-24).

Like Jim and Shirley, you may wonder how to encourage your child to show more interest in learning and help them develop their gifts and talents. Whether your child is currently thriving or floundering, I want to provide you with practical, biblically sound principles and strategies to help you raise kids who strive to do their best and know how to work hard. The first concept in the title of this chapter is *moxie*. Its traditional definition includes the qualities of courage, energy, determination, and skill. In essence, it means strength of character. The second concept in this title, *motivation*, is a quality that flows from having moxie. Although academic achievement can contribute to life success, our children's spiritual strength—demonstrated in part by their moxie and motivation—is the root of good character and a life pleasing to God (see Colossians 1:10).

WHAT DRIVES MOXIE AND MOTIVATION?

Toddlers and preschool-age children are naturally curious, often highly motivated to explore and experiment with just about everything around them. This is why parenting during the early ages can be so exhausting. It's also why childproof latches were invented to keep them out of cabinets! If your child has lost their God-given passion for exploration and learning, it's important to investigate the causes. Fortunately, no matter how unmotivated they may seem to be, you can take action to help them. This involves understanding how determination and intrinsic motivation—the desire to persevere, to learn, and to complete any task—can be derailed when kids are distracted by trying to meet deeper needs such as security, control, belonging, a sense of competence, and relationship. This also involves considering whether your well-intentioned attempts to motivate them may be backfiring.

Back to the Basics

Even the most God-loving families can face great stress due to financial challenges, illnesses, relocations, children with learning and developmental differences, and the inevitable conflicts of life. Some also experience far greater trials, such as job losses, serious accidents, natural disasters, significant mental health challenges, chronic marital conflict, divorce, or death. Obviously, any of these can lead to anxiety, fear, discouragement, and other painful emotions in parents and kids alike. Some even result in feelings so overwhelming that they activate the nervous system's fight-or-flight response, causing those impacted to habitually focus every aspect of their attention on immediate survival. In essence, the brain prioritizes the closest and most tangible source of perceived safety. While this can be healthy in the short term, it can lead just about anyone to fall into longer-term patterns of trying to meet their needs in ineffective or unhealthy ways rather than through a relationship with Christ. For example, a child who is experiencing feelings of loss due to parents who are divorcing may act out or engage in reckless behavior simply to be approved by the in-crowd and receive validation. A child bullied at school, seeking a sense of security or power, may become withdrawn and spend a lot of time daydreaming. Yet another child might behave in rebellious ways to seek the limits and supervision they so deeply crave. In each of these cases, the child prioritizes finding security rather than demonstrating moxie and motivation.

From my studies of countless families, I've seen that unmotivated children are often preoccupied with pursuing needs essential to physical, emotional, or spiritual survival. This leaves them with limited energy and confidence to take the necessary and healthy risks required to move beyond their immediate comfort zones and think beyond the present moment. It's important to emphasize that they are usually unaware of what is going on in their minds. As a result, they may be unable to choose a better behavior, express why they feel unmotivated, or ask for help.

In some instances, the reasons for unmet needs are obvious. When I was talking with a missionary serving a remote village in southern Asia, she described a five-year-old boy who was blind, homeless, and forced to beg to survive. Once he was placed in a loving home, this child began to receive the love, security, guidance, and physical nourishment he needed. Eventually, as he felt more secure and built bonds of trust with those caring for him, he demonstrated a strong desire to learn to read braille. His needs being met unlocked the passion for learning and growth that God had given him.

Unmotivated children are often preoccupied with pursuing needs essential to physical, emotional, or spiritual survival.

In other cases, unmet needs are not the result of such severe deprivation, but they can still have a significant impact on motivation. For example, many children with learning disabilities feel poorly about themselves. For these children, the motivation to zone out or misbehave is often greater than the motivation to work and persevere. Still others are so stressed by social media and other digital technology that they have little energy, confidence, or time to grow in healthy ways.

Regardless of the possible causes, the healthiest first step is to pause and pray. When we do, we are reminded that we are not alone in our struggles. We have a Savior, Jesus Christ, who is more than capable of empathizing with our struggles and our suffering (see Hebrews 4:15, NIV). He is also the Great Physician who is more than pleased when we humbly seek His help (see James 4:6). The following prayer is an example of how we might seek God's help:

Dear Lord, I feel overwhelmed. I feel afraid. I don't know what to do to help my child, but I trust You to show me. Please put godly people into my life who will help me understand what my child really needs and to meet these needs in ways that glorify You and exemplify Your Love for my child.

We need God's help, and we also need the help of other people who love Him. If your child is struggling with underachievement or any other complex challenge, please don't keep it a secret, trying to solve it without benefiting from the perspective and prayers of others. God has gifted many people with specialized skills and knowledge to help kids struggling with character challenges and lack of motivation.

> We don't have to understand every detail of what's causing our children to struggle before simply choosing to demonstrate our unconditional love for them.

Before discussing some common parenting pitfalls that diminish motivation, I want to emphasize that we don't have to understand every detail of what's causing our children to struggle before simply choosing to demonstrate our unconditional love for them. Love is powerful. Love meets a variety of the needs that cannot be met in any other way. Great things done without love will usually fail, and imperfect things done with it will likely have great benefit over time. As a wise person once told me, "Always err on the side of love."

Q & A: What Might You Do If Your Child Has Learning Differences?

Seeing your child struggle with learning differences can be discouraging, and you should not try to navigate through this experience alone. If you face this challenge, I hope to encourage you by offering some steps many families take to support their children in school and life.

1. **Surround yourself with supportive people.** Many parents in this situation become isolated. They are also at great risk for burnout. Connecting with parents, professionals, and teachers who understand your challenges and who care for you and your child can make a huge difference!

2. **Ask God to help you understand what your child truly needs.** Too often people ask the wrong question: "Will this work with my child given their unique needs?" A more effective question is "What specific supports and skills does my child need to succeed?"

3. **Teach, practice, reteach, and practice.** Repeat as needed. This is what God does with us. He knows that we need lots of instruction, lots of examples, lots of practice, and a huge amount of grace.

4. **See your child as capable.** Be a "they can" not a "they can't" parent. Kids tend to live up to or down to the expectations we have for them. Too frequently parents err on the side of setting very low ones. Wiser moms and dads err on the side of setting ones that might be a bit high. Then they teach, practice, and reteach the required skills, adjusting their expectations downward only when it becomes apparent that they are too high. I've known many parents who, through great love, hard work, and patience, helped their children succeed, despite learning differences and other challenges.

Parenting Pitfalls

Earlier, we looked at some of the problems associated with permissive, helicopter, and drill sergeant parents. When employed habitually, such approaches can also dampen our kids' motivation. As I mentioned, some children find it difficult to maintain focus because they lack the limits and loving discipline required to feel safe and loved. Others are so overcontrolled by their parents that they either rebel or resist through passive avoidance in an attempt to gain some sense of freedom.

Although we do want to encourage our kids and hold them accountable, the difficulty comes when we try to change two things that are beyond our *direct* control: (1) another person's strongly held attitudes and motivations, and (2) their inherent strengths and weaknesses. When our kids are uninterested, particularly if they are also unable to meet the standards we set, we won't get very far by constantly reminding them to do their homework, punishing them, or warning them about how hard life will be if they don't get a good education. In fact, the harder we try to force the issue, the less real progress we tend to see, and the more power struggles we encounter. We won't even make much long-term headway with more positive strategies such as providing praise, giving rewards, or offering frequent support. It quickly becomes clear that, though we might be able to hand-hold them into working for a short period of time, this does not guarantee they will have the moxie and motivation to continue when we aren't actively pushing them along.

Brenda, a longtime friend of ours, is a dedicated and successful middle school educator. She told my wife and me how she was struggling with her fifteen-year-old son. Will had never liked school, but he seemed a polite and compliant kid. Then Mrs. Ryder, his high school English teacher, called Brenda and told her, "Will hasn't been handing in his writing assignments. He's missing several essays required for him to pass my class."

Brenda decided to take matters into her own hands. Sitting with her son every night for two weeks, she ensured that he got the work done.

Two weeks later, she received another call from the teacher. "Will still hasn't handed in any papers," Mrs. Ryder reported.

Brenda was livid. "What?! I know he did them!"

The teacher continued, "I'm sorry to tell you this, but he hasn't handed them in."

That evening Brenda sat down with her son. "I saw you do those papers, but Mrs. Ryder called today and told me you still have not handed any of them in."

Looking at the floor, Will mumbled something under his breath.

"What?" said Brenda. "I can't hear you."

Now looking her straight in the eyes, he shared the truth. "Mom, you can make me do that stuff, but you can't make me turn it in."

Will had chosen to risk failing the class just to prove to his mother that he would not be coerced into doing what she demanded. Apparently he wasn't as compliant as she had assumed, and there was much more going on than him simply getting a little behind on his work.

FIVE STEPS TO BOOST YOUR CHILD'S MOTIVATION

As Brenda discovered, motivating kids isn't always as simple as making them do what we want. You've probably noticed that they have minds of their own! In fact, it is easy to get into power struggles with kids who are determined to do things their own way.

Let's start by remembering that God created humans to be curious and to learn, and to gain satisfaction from doing so. These gifts are a blessing, but they can also lead to trouble if we are not doing our part to lovingly yet firmly shape our children's character as early in life as possible. As I keep emphasizing, the solutions to underachievement require that we put character first.

Fortunately, there is no need to be overwhelmed by this as a parent. In the remainder of this chapter, I will discuss five practical steps you can take. In the process of applying these steps, you will help your children learn to be loving and godly people while also helping them become excited about learning, growing, and working hard:

- Evaluate your current approach to motivating your child.
- End any control battles as soon as possible.
- Make your kids responsible for their own learning, grades, and other obligations.
- Allow them to experience the blessings of struggling and serving.
- Encourage your children to discover and exercise their God-given gifts.

Step 1: Evaluate Your Current Approach to Motivating Your Child

As parents, we are wise to ask ourselves some important questions:

Are our kids growing in their ability to be personally accountable for their schoolwork and other responsibilities, or do we keep having to nag and remind them?

Are we frequently finding ourselves getting pulled into power struggles over their academic learning?

Are we seeing any growth in spiritual strength and behaviors that represent good character?

Answering these questions may help you realize that the lectures, reminders, warnings, rewards, and punishments you may be using to motivate your kids will offer only short-term benefits at best. You may even realize that doing these things is having an immediate *negative* impact, leading to a marked deterioration in the quality of your relationship with your kids. If this seems to be the case for you, it's time to focus on taking the following four steps.

Step 2: End Any Control Battles as Soon as Possible

It is neurologically impossible for the brain to focus on love, learning, or any other godly pursuit when it is distracted by power struggles. Without love, nothing valuable is accomplished.

> If I speak in the tongues of men or of angels, but do not have love, I am only a resounding gong or a clanging cymbal. If I have the gift of prophecy and can fathom all mysteries and all knowledge, and if I have a faith that can move mountains, but do not have love, I am nothing. If I give all I possess to the poor and give over my body to hardship that I may boast, but do not have love, I gain nothing.
>
> 1 CORINTHIANS 13:1-3, NIV

Frequent lectures, warnings, and reminders tend to have two unfortunate results:

- conflict escalates, damaging the parent-child relationship, and
- children become dependent upon being lectured, warned, or reminded to do their work.

One mother put it well: "My daughter has become a 'reminder addict.' The more I give, the more she seems to need."

There's good news! It only takes one person to end a power struggle. Eliminating frequent reminders will also help your child learn to need fewer of them. The following dialogue provides an example of how a parent might begin this process. Remember that the adult's tone of voice should always be calm, sincere, and caring.

Parent: I've been doing something that's not helpful, and I want to apologize.
Child: What?
Parent: I've been spending way too much time reminding you to do your schoolwork and other things that you are responsible for. I've done this because I love you and want to see you do well, but it's making things worse.
Child: Yeah, I hate it when you nag me. Besides, it's my life.
Parent: Yes, it is your life. You get to decide how you live it. That's why I am going to stop nagging.
Child: So I can do whatever I want?
Parent: Each of us can do whatever we want, but we must be ready for both good and bad consequences.
Child: Well, I just hate school!
Parent: That must make it really hard. We love you and are here to help in any way we can.

Having this conversation can be scary for some parents. One father questioned, "Does this mean that I am going to allow my kid to fail? I don't know if I can do that."

I replied with two questions of my own. "Does God allow us the freedom to fail? If so, why is that?"

This father replied, "Yes, He does. I think it's because He wants us to learn for ourselves and choose what is good rather than being forced into it."

"He lets us fail so we can see that it's better to trust and follow Him," I agreed. "For most of us, isn't experiencing the consequences of poor decisions what really motivates us to make better ones?"

"It's hard as a parent," he admitted, "but when I think about it that way, I know giving up control is the right thing to do."

Step 3: Make Your Kids Responsible for Their Own Learning, Grades, and Other Obligations

Just prior to beginning college, I worked part-time at a discount rental car company. My job was to clean and refuel each vehicle once it was returned. Of course, I was also expected to check for damage and report it promptly to my supervisor. It probably won't surprise you to hear that those vehicles were often returned with plenty of bumps and bruises. Lamenting how poorly the cars were treated, I once asked my supervisor why people were so careless with them. His response was brief, yet memorable: "It's because they don't own them."

Too often, children have "rental car" lives. They don't take care of them because they don't own them. They don't own them because they too often don't have to own the consequences of their choices. Deep down, they think, *I can do whatever I want with this life. The choices I make don't really matter. Somebody will always remind me or rescue me from the consequences.*

Stepping out of the helicopter or drill sergeant styles can be scary. What is likely to happen when we begin to truly allow our kids to be responsible for their grades without rescuing or micromanaging them?

Will things improve right away, or might they worsen first?

Typically speaking, parents report rapid improvement in the relationship they have with their child. Since they are not fighting control battles, there are fewer arguments and blowups over homework, schoolwork, and grades.

What doesn't immediately improve is their child's academic achievement, motivation, and performance. In fact, many report an immediate yet temporary decline in these areas. Why? First, children who are used to having others own their learning often lack the habits required to take responsibility for this area. This often becomes apparent only after their parents take their hands off the steering wheel and allow them to really drive their own lives.

There is another reason for this temporary decline in performance. When we allow them to own their academic choices, kids often need to test two things: First, they test the limits of their own freedom. The question *How far can I push this?* bounces around in their minds. Second, many will need to test our sincerity, wondering, *Are my parents really serious about this? Are they willing to stick with this, or will they go back to their old ways?*

When parents respond to this dip in performance with sadness *for their child*, rather than anger *at them*, a very healthy message is sent: "I love you and am very concerned about what you will go through as a result of your poor decision." This keeps the focus on the child's poor decision rather than parents' emotions.

Parents also tend to ask, "What type of consequences should we provide when our children are not putting reasonable effort into their academics?" Before I answer, notice the phrase *reasonable effort.* When it comes to grades, we need to place most of our emphasis on kids' level of effort and the quality of their hearts rather than their grades themselves. Some children, regardless of how hard they work and how much academic help they're given, will not be capable of the same academic success as others. Wise parents recognize this and adjust their expectations appropriately, always erring on the side of teaching and guiding.

Even in the case of kids who are making little or no effort in school, it's helpful to view our guidance as a way of gently yet firmly teaching them how the real world works rather than punishing them. Remember, at this point in their lives, the consequences are still relatively small.

Let's see what this might look like with a child who is around ten or older. As you read the following conversation, please remember that this scenario involves a child who was capable of success but chose not to exert much effort. He earned bad grades because he repeatedly decided to play rather than display a reasonable level of moxie. Notice how his parents speak to him with a tone of sincere concern and empathy, not anger or sarcasm.

Mother: Your dad and I just looked over your report card and noticed that several of your grades dropped a lot this semester. We love you, so we aren't going to freak out or yell at you.
Father: That's right. We do love you, and we are mostly concerned about how we might help you do better. That's why we have always offered you a lot of help. Do you have any idea why you haven't accepted this help?
Son: Well, I don't know.
Father: I think it might be that your mom and I haven't given you a good picture of what it takes to earn the things you have.
Son: Well, what does that mean?
Mom: We are concerned that we are giving you things right now that you won't be able to afford as an adult if you don't learn better work habits.
Son: That's not true.
Mom: We don't want you to become an adult and be surprised by how hard it is to earn a comfortable life.
Father: Yes, that's why we are happy to let you play baseball and provide other privileges, but it's important that you do your best in school, help around the house, and do the other things we ask of you. This is how it works for adults, and it's our job to help you learn this before you become one. For now, you'll need to find a way to pay for your baseball jersey and some of the other nonessentials you've been wanting.

Son: But that's not fair!
Mother: Son, we love you too much to fight and argue with you about this.
Father: That's right. We will feel better about providing you with the extras you want when we see that you are doing your best by working hard.

This conversation may seem harsh to some, but consider the fact that in the blink of an eye your children will be adults, facing life in a world that is built around stark economic principles, not the grace you have for them in your heart. Should you assign them responsibility when they are older and the consequences are large, or as soon as possible while the consequences are still relatively small? I believe the kindest thing you can do is teach them now. Of course, this does not mean being legalistic or harsh. It means allowing them to face the realities of life in a gradual and loving, yet firm and real way.

Step 4: Allow Them to Experience the Blessings of Struggling and Serving

In recent decades, researchers have provided alarming statistics pertaining to the percentages of young people who leave the faith by age thirty:

> We estimate that 31% of people raised Christian become unaffiliated between ages 15 to 29, the tumultuous period in which religious switching is concentrated. An additional 7% of people raised Christian become unaffiliated later in life, after the age of 30.[1]

While the reasons for their departure from organized Christian religion are varied, is it possible that a large proportion of these young people never truly owned their faith? Could it be that, rather than truly struggling and experiencing their need for Christ, they were always able to rely on faith only in their parents' provision?

Again, once brought to Christ by His grace alone, our kids do not automatically walk with Him like "spiritual" people. The path for every person is a personal and very narrow route full of struggles (see Matthew 7:14). All of us occasionally trip, stumble, and hit the ground hard enough to feel great sorrow and pain. From a spiritual perspective, this can be a great blessing. As parents, however, it's extremely hard to watch our children grow through this process. It's even more painful, though, to see them fail.

This is what can happen when we try to own their lives and their faith, rather than allowing them to see that God is their sustainer and strength. Perhaps the true question we must ask ourselves is this:

Do I really trust Christ to safely and lovingly lead my children through the valley of the shadow of death, or do I think He needs my help?

Our desire to "rescue" our kids from discomfort can also take the form of never expecting them to serve inside and outside of our homes. This is one of the most common impediments to the development of moxie in modern America. I remember talking with a couple about their middle schooler's academic underachievement. When I asked them about the types of things their son was expected to do to exercise his character, they looked surprised. "What do you mean?" they asked.

I replied with a few questions: "Does he serve the family by doing chores and other things that benefit others? How about service in the community? Does he do any form of volunteer work that requires him to sacrifice some time and energy?"

Both of them stared at me as if I were from another planet.

Glancing at each other and back my way, they both told me he was just too busy.

Trying to understand, I queried further. "What do you mean? What sorts of things are causing him to be too busy for these things?"

Mom answered first. "He has a lot of homework, his soccer schedule is very demanding, and we feel that he needs time to connect with his friends online."

"Yes, the homework is a big deal," Dad added. "It seems like it takes him forever. And did we tell you about his piano lessons?"

"So what you are saying is that his homework takes a very long time to complete. He also has soccer practice and games and is taking piano lessons," I said. "Do I have all of this right?"

Both of them nodded.

"I wonder how he is getting his needs met for honor, service, and sacrifice," I said.

The room became silent.

Dad was the first to speak up. "What do you mean?"

"There's no doubt that the priorities you have for your son are very good," I explained. "He is learning valuable skills and some good lessons about work and perseverance. Still, how important are grades, sports, music, and connecting with friends online compared to learning how to honor, serve, and sacrifice for others?"

There is no doubt that academics are important. There is also great value in kids participating in extracurricular activities led by people who understand that their primary role is to demonstrate and teach service and other good character attributes. Many children come to Christ and grow spiritually through participation in church camps, teams, and other activities that are centered around the gospel. In our culture, however, parents, coaches, and other youth leaders often allow character and spiritual development to take a back seat to academics, sports, and other activities. As a result, kids spend most of their time being served rather than learning to serve. Again, I want to make it clear that these activities are wonderful when provided within the goal of first teaching service and other character attributes. When they are not, some sad things begin to happen:

- Kids come to believe that how good they are at something is more important than how well they treat other people. This is a recipe for pride, as they look down on others who they view as being less knowledgeable.
- Parents often begin to slip into the habit of giving a pass on poor character as long as their kids are doing well in school.
- Many people entering the workforce possess great transcripts yet lack the skills employers desire the most, including work ethic, humility, patience, teamwork, and reliability.
- Kids can miss out on important opportunities to exercise their faith by making sacrifices that benefit others.
- Many young people develop an "It's all about me" attitude.

I write this from a place of experience. I personally know how much pressure is felt by parents to make sure that their children are good students and constantly involved in a variety of activities. I also know how subtle yet powerful this temptation grows over time when someone very gradually yet consistently puts character and spiritual matters on the back burner. I'm not proud of this, but it's important that I be honest. It's also important that you know that it is never too late to start making changes.

The place to begin is ensuring that your kids are contributing to the family by doing chores and aren't consistently avoiding this responsibility by claiming they have too much homework or other "important" things to do. While it's wise to apply common sense, grace, and a bit of flexibility, serving the family must remain a priority. There was a time in history when getting an education, even as a child, was regarded as a privilege that few could enjoy. This is still the case in many if not most parts of the world. Even now, when an education is framed as a special privilege and opportunity to rise above one's circumstances, kids often pursue it with greater enthusiasm.

In chapter 6, I discussed the importance of chores and how we can train our children to do them. I also addressed why it's so important for kids to be involved in service to others outside of the home. Finally, I recommended that kids be expected to work for most of the extras they desire. Applying those concepts will help you lovingly build responsibility in your kids without getting mired in unwinnable arguments and power struggles. Few things limit motivation more than knowing that all the perks of success are available without having to exert any of the sweat normally associated with earning them. This pattern is far too common in families, even those where the parents must scrimp and do without so that they can buy their children what they want.

When an education is framed as a special privilege and opportunity to rise above one's circumstances, kids often pursue it with greater enthusiasm.

Parents who place a high priority on academic excellence often believe that it's better for their children to devote themselves to their education than be distracted by working part-time jobs. Of course, there may be times when a young person's studies require more time and energy than others. Nevertheless, there are few activities that will teach them more about the realities of life than doing hard work.

As a teen and young adult, I was blessed to have parents who understood this. I knew that if I wanted something extra, I had to find a way to earn it. Because of this, I had many instructive and motivating jobs as a youth. One involved working as a busboy and dishwasher at a restaurant near our home. The place was always

Balancing Sports and Other Activities with Your Kids' Spiritual Development

Kids who play sports, learn a musical instrument, spend time with their friends, and do other fun activities are learning valuable life skills. It's even more important, though, that we guide them toward doing such things with God as the clear centerpiece of their lives: "Whatever you do, work heartily, as for the Lord and not for men" (Colossians 3:23). In this way, they learn to integrate their faith and spiritual growth with everything they do.

From a practical perspective, how can we as parents achieve a healthy balance in which we teach our children to worship and honor God as they enjoy the good things that He provides?

- **Encourage your children to view participation as a form of ministry.** Teach them that God is the source of life, as well as the source of all of their abilities. Be sure to establish high expectations for how your children will behave while participating. I consider the following rule essential: "In all that we do, we represent God with integrity, honor, and love toward others."

- **Remember that saying no to good things is okay and often important.** Early in my career, I discovered that many families fall into conflict, unhappiness, and chaos not because they are doing a multitude of obviously sinful things. Instead, they have allowed themselves to be pulled into too many *good* activities. God does not want your family to run yourselves ragged, drive yourselves into unnecessary financial stress, or be distracted spiritually because your kids are constantly involved in extra activities.

- **Remember that no person is immune to pride and its awful consequences.** As the parent of three boys, I found myself struggling with an insidious form of temptation. It started when a coach, music teacher, or other kind adult shared enthusiasm about my child's performance or potential talent. Quite naturally this left me feeling proud of my son and pretty good about myself as his dad. I was fortunate that someone I respected loved me and my family enough to help me see that I was slipping into unhealthy thinking. As I discovered, it is natural to take pride in our kids' achievements, but when we do so, we can begin to put more emphasis on maintaining these good feelings than on leading our children toward God.

- **Lean toward demonstrating grace.** There is a difference between having high and healthy expectations for godly behavior and having unrealistic, perfectionistic ones. Some parents make the tragic mistake of pressuring their children to be the best in every activity they pursue. (The same goes, of course, for some coaches, teachers, and other activity leaders.) This approach is completely inconsistent with the gospel of grace, and it will discourage children from following our spiritual lead. Dads—and mothers too—remember this warning: "Fathers, do not provoke your children, lest they become discouraged" (Colossians 3:21).

  It is healthy for our children to be challenged and lovingly held accountable for their choices. It is immeasurably destructive for them to experience a continuous stream of criticism and shame.

understaffed and swamped with customers, so it was surprisingly intense, exhausting, and dirty work. Another job involved helping pour and finish concrete foundations and floors. That was heavy work! From these and many other experiences, I developed lasting respect and appreciation for people who do the many difficult and not-so-glamorous jobs that benefit us all. I also learned to tolerate tedium and struggle: two situations we must all be able to endure at times.

One of the greatest gifts we can give our children is the ability to experience contentment not only in times of abundance and ease but also when life becomes dull or difficult. We do so not by depriving them of what they need, treating them harshly, or actively trying to make their lives difficult. Instead, we accomplish this by demonstrating great compassion and care as we gradually allow them to assume more real-life responsibilities. While doing so we pray that they will discover the strength that is found only in Christ: "I can do all things through him who strengthens me" (Philippians 4:13).

Step 5: Encourage Your Children to Discover and Exercise Their God-Given Gifts

I began this chapter by describing a young boy who struggled in school, often choosing to act out and be sent to the principal's office rather than work through math and other subjects he found so difficult. Desperate for help, his parents, Jim and Shirley, talked with a child psychiatrist named Dr. Foster Cline.

"Our son has always had a more difficult time in school than his two older sisters," Shirley told him. "Even in kindergarten, he seemed to have a harder time with numbers. Math has never been his strong suit. He also seems so distracted, and he forgets things so quickly."

Jim agreed. "That's true. He's never liked school, and he really does seem to struggle with it. What worries me most is that it seems like he is starting to give up."

Shirley nodded. "He's going to school every day, but it's like he's already started to drop out. He's only in the fourth grade."

"What's he good at?" Dr. Cline inquired.

"He's a good reader," Jim replied. "He's crazy about cars and other mechanical things. Give him a book about those, and he won't put it away until he's read it all."

"Yes," Shirley agreed, "and he likes to read about other things too. Last week he finished a book on reptiles. He can also tell you just about anything you might want to know about sharks."

"The problem," said Jim, "is that all the other reading gets in the way of his work on math."

"Help me understand," replied Dr. Cline. "It seems like being good at reading and doing a lot of it is good."

"Well, it is," Jim clarified, "but the school has emphasized that we should put our focus on the problems he's having with math. I guess it makes sense. I mean there's only a limited amount of time. Shouldn't we emphasize the subjects where he needs more help?"

"So you have been putting most of your emphasis on his problems?" Dr. Cline asked.

"Yes, math has been the focus," Shirley answered.

"What are some other things your son likes and is good at?" Dr. Cline asked.

"He likes art and music," Shirley answered with a smile.

Jim added, "If we let him, he'd spend most of the day drawing and playing his trombone. He loves both, and he's pretty good at them too."

"May I ask both of you a question?" Dr. Cline inquired.

"Of course."

"How excited would the two of you be about learning and life if you were required to focus almost solely on what you found to be the most difficult?"

They were silent.

Dr. Cline interrupted the pause with a question: "May I ask you something else?"

Both nodded.

"How would you begin to feel about yourselves," the doctor inquired gently, "if you were required to focus on what you find hardest every day?"

On the verge of tears, Shirley answered, "Horrible. I would feel horrible."

"That wouldn't work for me," Jim said, "but how are we supposed to help him if we don't focus mostly on math and other things that are hard for him? Besides, this is what the school told us that we needed to do."

"In my training as a child psychiatrist," said Dr. Cline, "I was taught to find out what a child has problems with and help them improve in those areas. Teachers are trained to do the same thing. Sometimes this is necessary, but doing too much of it can cause everyone to lose sight of the bigger picture. God gives each person at least one gift. As parents it is our job to help our kids discover these gifts and learn how to use them for the good of others. It doesn't mean we don't help them improve in areas that are difficult for them. It simply means that we shouldn't put our exclusive focus on these things. Besides, successful people put most of their energy into growing in their gifts."

"I don't think it's the school's intention, but it's almost like we feel guilty for not dwelling on the problems he is having," Shirley admitted.

"Yes," Jim replied, "we don't want to let him down."

"What if he never became much better at math," asked Dr. Cline, "but you taught him how to excel at what he is good at and he became a really good man?"

Relieved, Jim answered, "Oh, that would be great!"

"Yes, that would be amazing!" Shirley exclaimed.

In today's highly competitive educational and occupational environments, conscientious parents and educators experience tremendous pressure to help their children and students excel in all areas. With this pressure comes the tendency to ignore the following facts:

- Very few people are gifted in every area of life.
- Few things are more demotivating than dwelling on one's weaknesses.
- The most successful people focus the majority of their time and energy on what they do well.
- Our kids are more likely to be willing to grow in their areas of weakness when we build them up in their areas of strength.
- Many highly successful people have chosen a career in the trades or some other field that does not require a traditional college education.
- Character and faith are more important than anything else.

There are two categories of gifts. The first are spiritual gifts, those unique abilities empowered by the Holy Spirit for the purpose of building up the church (see, for example, Romans 12:6-8; 1 Corinthians 12:4-11; and 1 Corinthians 12:28). The second are natural abilities also given to us by God for the benefit of serving others and reflecting His glory.

You can help your kids identify their true gifts by asking two questions:

> "What do you enjoy doing so much that you want to do it most of the time?"

When asked this question, most children and teens describe how they love playing with their dog, enjoying time with friends, playing video games, reading, drawing, playing music, watching videos, and engaging in other fun activities. While these activities may be enjoyable and kids may be good at them, they do not necessarily qualify as gifts. Why? The second question reveals the answer:

> "How does doing this thing that you are good at and enjoy also benefit others?"

A true gift is something our children find natural and enjoyable to do *and* helps others in some way. God gives gifts so that we may bless others. "And God is able to make all grace abound to you, so that having all sufficiency in all things at all times, you may abound in every good work" (2 Corinthians 9:8). When our children are encouraged to pursue their gifts with the purpose of blessing others, they are learning to seek first the Kingdom of God.

Jim and Shirley began encouraging their son to pursue his love of reading, mechanics, and music. Instead of focusing on his struggles with numbers, they spent most of their time celebrating what he enjoyed reading about and learning at school and in his free time. As they did, they often repeated the same encouragement: "Our prayer for you is that you will find a way to use your gifts to help others. If you do, you will have a happy and rewarding life."

Dr. Cline had helped Jim and Shirley evaluate their approach while trying to motivate their son. Next he worked with them on putting together a plan to work through the other four steps. They ended the control battle; allowed their son to take ownership of his learning and grades; emphasized character and spiritual growth; and encouraged him to discover and exercise his God-given gifts.

As the years passed, Jim and Shirley prayed for the strength to stick with their plan. As you might imagine, their son's schooling didn't always go smoothly. What they did see, however, was continued growth in the quality of their relationship with him, the strength of his character, and his mechanical skills. In his final year of high school, he started his career in the automotive field, repairing cars for others in their small community. After graduating, he quickly landed a job as a mechanic at a new car dealership in a bigger city. Soon, he was loving his work and making a decent living.

Jim and Shirley's son continued to read, and he became fascinated with science and psychology. It wasn't long before he started wondering, *What would I have to do to become a psychologist?* It seemed like a crazy thought, but it just wouldn't go away. Because the idea kept bouncing around in his head, he took a couple classes at a local community college. Much to his surprise, he earned A's in both. As a result, he signed up for more. Once again, he did well. After nearly a decade of study, he had completed his doctoral degree with highest honors.

By now perhaps you have guessed: I am Jim and Shirley's son. I was that boy who struggled with serious learning challenges.

Every child is different. Some find school relatively simple. Others find it difficult. Some are given certain gifts, and some are given others. Common to all is the God-given drive to explore, learn, and grow. My prayer for your children is that they would be free to grow in the direction that God desires for their lives, always remembering the following: "Every good gift and every perfect gift is from above, coming down from the Father of lights, with whom there is no variation or shadow due to change" (James 1:17).

God is always good and generous. Although we may be surprised by how this shows up in the gifts and personalities of our kids, He never fails to amaze and astonish us with His grace.

CHAPTER 9

SMART STRATEGIES AROUND SMARTPHONES AND SCREENS

Helping Your Kids Develop a Healthy Relationship with Technology

"All my friends have phones," ten-year-old Jada pleaded. "I don't see why you won't let me have one. Besides, how am I supposed to get ahold of you if I need help?"

Jada's parents, Ben and Naomi, were conflicted. Their minds raced with thoughts like these: *It does seem most of her friends have phones. What if there is some sort of emergency, and she needs to reach us? Yeah, but it seems like so many kids are getting involved in way too many unhealthy things online. We could get her one that doesn't connect to the internet, but then she'd be excluded from using social media with her friends. She's already told us how humiliating that would be. Is it really as dangerous as some people say it is? What should we do?*

I wish they could have talked with Ron and Sumi, who had faced this same dilemma three years earlier when their son, Wyatt, was eleven. At that time they got him his first smartphone, reasoning that it would really be helpful as a way to track him. Their son was a good kid, and they reasoned that it would be better to give him a smartphone rather than argue about it all the time. They also knew he needed access to the scheduling apps his coaches used for baseball and soccer. Just to be safe, they decided to set the parent controls so he couldn't view inappropriate content.

Looking back, Wyatt's parents regret not waiting. He now spends most of his time staring at his phone, watching videos, texting, and getting drawn into drama with a girl from youth group at church. When talking with me about it, Sumi said, "Wyatt is on a constant emotional roller coaster—way worse than the normal ups and downs that teens go through."

"It's scary," Ron agreed. "He's almost always irritable and has become disrespectful. His poor attitude definitely corresponds with how much he uses his phone or other devices. He seems to be incredibly addicted to being online. When we tried to take away his phone, he started using his video game console to access the internet. We had no idea he could do that!"

These parents' stories illustrate the complexity parents face as they make decisions about when and how to allow kids access to technology while seeking to raise healthy, spiritually strong kids.

In this chapter, I will briefly discuss some of the dangers and benefits of this technology. Then I will give you a clear road map that cuts through the confusion and empowers you to follow the specific and very achievable steps required to protect and guide your kids. By taking these actions, you will help your children develop the values and virtues required to make healthy choices about how they use social media, the internet, and digital technology in general. These measures will also help you preserve your relationship with your kids and point them toward the authentic relationship they can have with Jesus Christ.

NAVIGATING THE DIGITAL WORLD

If you are concerned about the type of relationship your child develops with digital technology, you are very wise. The risks are well documented and can impact any family. It's safe to assume that you've heard horror stories about adult sex predators posing as youth or of young people being bullied or harassed online, sometimes so relentlessly that they have chosen to end their lives. You probably have a good idea of how addictive video games, social media, and other digital activities are. You likely know that a lot of online content runs completely counter to the Christian values and behaviors you want your kids to adopt. In fact, the digital world is full of material representing the "seven deadly sins": lust, gluttony, greed, sloth, wrath, envy, and pride.

Aside from these obvious downsides, smartphones and other digital technologies can keep our kids from exploring the wider world in real life. In fact, learning requires active engagement with creation. God uses His beautiful creation to teach us and to bring glory to Himself. As little children, we begin to learn big lessons about God and His ways by interacting with what He has made. We learn about gravity by running, playing, and occasionally falling. We discover that sand runs through our fingers when we try to hold on to it too tightly. We feel joy when we hear birds sing, and we feel astonishment when we discover how hard it is to catch a butterfly or watch ants carry things much bigger than themselves.

Technology may also interfere with how young people connect and build relationships with others and God. It may dampen their desire to explore the gifts He has given them and live into their potential. The world is God's classroom, and our kids' brains and bodies grow strong as they interact with real people and things they can see, hear, smell, and touch.

It is sobering to note that the very nature of any effective social marketing campaign hinges on its ability to convince us that we have a problem we didn't realize we had or that we lack something we need to make us happy. These outside forces seek to create discontentment so we will go after the shiny object or idea that they are selling. Of course, well before computer chips, wireless networks, and artificial intelligence, Adam and Eve succumbed to this subtle yet powerful form of deception.

At this point you may be thinking, *Wow! Those are some bold statements. Technology, digital media, and marketing aren't all bad. It's not like the devil is lurking behind every screen or URL.*

Actually, you are correct. That's what makes this such a challenging and potentially confusing subject. Because digital technology is such an important part of our world with many wonderful benefits, we have little choice about whether or not our children eventually will have a relationship with it. Starting in the early grades, many schools now require that assignments be completed and submitted online. Gone are the days when most families had a heavy set of encyclopedias resting on a shelf in the living room. Now kids usually need to go online to get the information they need to complete papers and other assignments. Coaches are communicating and scheduling with young players online, often using a variety of convenient apps. If our children aren't well versed in technology by the time they are older teens and young adults, their educational and career opportunities will be dramatically limited.

The benefits for adults can be great too. I recently made a repair on my car using step-by-step instructions I found in an online video. That saved me nearly $4,000. This reminded me that I really do like technology! Also, thanks to digital tools, the gospel is being preached to the ends of the earth as never before. Believers around the world now have access to church websites, Bible study aids, and countless translations of God's Word on their phones.

Without all these advantages, parenting around technology issues would be so much easier. We could just say no to anything with a computer chip, screen, and connectivity. Doing that, however, would deprive our kids of the ability to thrive in our modern world. It would also lead to rebellion and a missed opportunity to teach our kids the attitudes and skills they need to make good choices.

Dear reader, I wish I knew how to make raising kids in this digital age simple. I don't. This reminds us of our utter dependence on God in making the decisions required to raise the children He has given us. The only real solutions are found in a relationship with Jesus Christ and by following the same timeless truths He has taught from the beginning. The solution is relationship: relationship with Him and relationship between parent and child. Remember this: *Our children's relationship with technology is strongly impacted by our relationship with them. In order for us to successfully apply the strategies I discuss later in this chapter, we must first be building a strong and loving relationship of trust with our kids. Otherwise, they will grow in rebellion rather than responsibility when we provide the limits, supervision, and accountability they need to successfully navigate the world of technology.*

> Our children's relationship with technology is strongly impacted by our relationship with them.

Kids who feel secure and deeply loved by their parents are far less likely to seek fulfillment in unhealthy relationships of any kind.[1] They are less prone to become dependent upon drugs, alcohol, pornography, promiscuity, unhealthy peer relationships, endless hours spent playing video games, and other very unhealthy behaviors. This doesn't guarantee they will be perfect. In fact, they might make some very costly mistakes. However, it's far less likely they will further trap themselves by refusing to take responsibility and accept help.

Liam, Tony's twenty-year-old son, had always been a respectful, kind kid who seemed to love God from an early age. In his late teens, however, Liam started viewing pornography online. Not long after that, he received an email threatening to reveal what he was doing to his family and everyone else if he didn't pay an exorbitant amount of money. Liam was so anxious and depressed that he approached his dad and admitted what he'd gotten involved in. He also confessed that he was consumed by thoughts of ending his own life.

The therapist who helped Tony and his son navigate this horrible ordeal emphasized what a miracle it was that the young man had come to his father for help. As time passed and Liam overcame his addiction, the relationship between father and son grew even stronger. So did their relationships with Jesus.

PARENTAL GUIDANCE SUGGESTED

In the early 1970s, the Motion Picture Association of America began asking moviemakers to apply the PG rating to films with content that might not be suitable for children. That designation let parents know they should carefully consider whether to allow their children to see the movie. Nowadays, parental controls and other electronic safeguards on digital devices provide a similar function, but they are no substitute for solid, hands-on parenting.

Once when leading a workshop at a large church in San Jose, California, I met with a small group of parents who were also successful leaders in the tech industry. They worked in the heart of Silicon Valley, and many were programmers, website developers, and social media consultants. I asked them, "From your perspective, what are the most important things parents can do to keep their kids safe and help them learn to use technology in healthy ways?"

As a group, they began to make a list, which included these key points:

- Build positive relationships with your kids.
- Teach them values.

- Spend a lot of time doing fun things with them that do not require screens.
- Talk with kids about the risks of technology.
- Set limits, including keeping kids off cell phones and social media until they are older teens.
- Avoid being helicopter parents.
- Allow kids to learn from small mistakes, and hold them accountable with reasonable consequences.

They emphasized one point above all:

- Model healthy digital behavior.

Their answers were not what I expected. Because they were all experts in digital technology, I assumed they would prioritize the use of parental controls, content blockers, and other electronic safeguards. Interestingly, those didn't even make their list! I asked why. One of them, a seasoned tech executive and the parent of two teenagers, said something powerful: "Yes, digital controls and safeguards are very important. Every parent should research them and make sure that the most current are installed and correctly enabled on every device in their home. The problem is that they can provide a false sense of security."

> Digital controls and safeguards can provide a false sense of security.

I urged him to explain. In a serious tone, he used the example of a plane that crashed while landing at the San Francisco airport. After an investigation, the National Transportation Safety Board determined that the pilots had been too reliant on automated flight management systems. During this landing, the crew ran into many unpredicted circumstances, became fatigued, and ran out of time to react because they may have been too focused on the electronics.[2]

"That's tragic," I agreed, "but what does this have to do with kids and technology?"

"I know many parents who believe that since they've installed electronic safeguards, they don't have to be vigilant or involved with their kids over the issue," he said. Then he told me about a friend's thirteen-year-old daughter who was engaging in an inappropriate text-messaging relationship with her boyfriend. Since the electronic safeguards on her device indicated that all was well, these parents continued to take an extremely hands-off approach with her, putting little effort into maintaining a close relationship, setting reasonable limits, or providing good supervision. As a result, the very explicit sexual messaging continued for months because she had been using an old phone her boyfriend had given her.

If you reflect on your family's screen time habits and want to move in a healthier direction, please know that it's never too late to change. God's grace is amazing! You and your kids have access to this grace every day: "The steadfast love of the LORD never ceases; his mercies never come to an end; they are new every morning; great is your faithfulness" (Lamentations 3:22-23).

When it comes to digital technology, we as parents need all the help we can get. We need timely electronic safeguards, but more than anything we need the timeless relationship principles included in God's Word. Given how critical it is that parents build strong bonds with their very young children, we'll consider the reasons why it is especially important that young kids spend as little time as possible in front of screens. Then we'll look at how to carefully introduce technology to older children. Finally, we'll examine which biblical principles apply when we need to set more limits with a child who is making poor decisions while using technology.

THE PRESCREEN YEARS

During their first six years of life, children should have as little exposure to screens as is practically possible. This recommendation is not intended to be applied in a legalistic, extremely rigid, or unthinking manner. For example, if a loved one is away and only able to interact with a young child via a video call, this should be allowed. Occasionally showing a young child pictures on your device or viewing brief videos with them as part of a conversation between the two of you is fine. The goal, however, is to make screens as rare an experience in the lives of young children as possible, never allowing any device to assume the role of babysitter.

Why do I take such a strong stance on this subject? I believe that between their conception and about age six, children learn roughly 75 percent of the visual-perceptual, social-emotional, motor, cognitive, and behavioral competencies they will acquire during their lifetimes. This learning happens only when young children receive or experience

- eye contact, smiles, and loving touch;
- adequate physical nourishment;
- physical movement, first by being gently rocked and then by learning to crawl, toddle, run, jump, skip, and engage in other movements that require balance and hand-eye coordination;
- being talked to, read to, and listened to by adults and other children;
- working through small problems such as putting on clothing, coloring inside the lines, doing simple puzzles, waiting in line at the store, being expected to share, and being told no;
- helping others complete simple tasks like washing dishes, folding laundry, raking leaves, watering plants, setting the table, and dusting baseboards.

The brain develops in a use-it-or-lose-it fashion. At birth the infant brain already has about one hundred billion neurons.[3] During the first year outside the womb, the number of synapses, or connections between these neurons, explodes in number. Interestingly, starting around age two, the number of these connections begins to *decrease* through a process called synaptic pruning. By age ten, children have approximately half as many as they had at age one.[4] As a result of this pruning, neural connections that aren't used are eliminated. Those synapses strengthened through repeated use are retained.

Young children whose neurological structures adapt to a world full of healthy movement, human interactions, problem-solving, creativity, and biblical teachings develop brains attuned to these things. Those whose neurological structures adapt solely to watching and being entertained by screens become skilled primarily at those two functions. Despite what some advertisers say, I don't believe in the educational benefits of videos, video games, and other screen content for babies and preschoolers.

If your children are still very young, especially if you have more than one running around the house, you may be thinking, *What do I do instead? If I don't let my little ones have my phone or tablet, they go bonkers. How will I get my shopping done? What do I do when I'm trying to cook a meal, and they are crying like crazy or getting into everything?*

To be honest, I believe much of parenting during early childhood comes down to simply trying to get though chaotic-feeling situations without losing it by yelling or resorting to begging, bribing, pleading, or allowing them to stare at a screen. While that doesn't mean we should give up on doing everything we can to teach our kids good values, we should be suspicious of anyone claiming that they have some strategy or system that will make parenting little ones simple and easy.

The Boredom Training Session

Never in history have we had more access to stimulating sights, sounds, and activities. Because of this, many of us have either forgotten or never learned how to feel comfortable with monotony. When a moment of boredom hits, we quickly go to our phone, tablet, or other device for a quick dose of stimulation. Kids are no different. In fact, many of them view being bored as one of the most terrible experiences known to humankind.

Many years ago, I found myself pondering these ideas and reflecting on my own struggles as a parent. As a result, I wrote a brief article titled "Don't Raise an Entertainment Junkie." In it I suggested that parents provide what I call "Boredom Training Sessions." The suggestions I provided were intended to be a lighthearted, slightly humorous look at how we might raise kids who see boredom as an opportunity for creative thought rather than a horrible curse to be avoided like the plague. I even provided action steps parents could apply once their children were about three years of age. I knew the ideas were solid, but I didn't honestly believe that many would apply them. Much to my surprise, countless parents did, and quite a few have commented on the positive impact the process made on their families and children.

Four Steps for the Boredom Training Session

Step 1: Find strategic times for your child to become bored. Wise parents pick times when they know they will have the patience and strength to remain firm instead of getting angry or giving in to boredom-related fits.

Parents are also smart to consider the length of unstructured time that seems best given their children's age and ability. Some start with a period lasting no more than five or ten minutes. Others go for longer durations. The goal is to start with something attainable and gradually increase the length as they become better able to entertain themselves. Of course, the goal of doing this is not to ignore our children but to create a healthier balance where they get plenty of attention but also learn how to be content without it.

Step 2: Provide simple items and activities they can use to keep themselves occupied. Examples include crayons, paper, a cardboard box, easy puzzles, dolls, toy cars, and other simple toys. Even better is sending them outside to play in a pile of sand or with some pine cones, sticks, and other elements of God's creation.

Without a doubt, allowing our children to become bored does not mean we are not supervising them. Their safety is always our top priority.

Step 3: Gently yet firmly teach your child to learn that they can handle being bored. You've surely noticed a theme running through this book: Every challenge a child encounters is an opportunity for them to learn and to grow physically, mentally, emotionally, and spiritually. This is precisely why they need to occasionally experience boredom and find ways to cope with it rather than expect someone to come to the rescue with something exciting.

In chapter 7 I shared five steps for guiding children to own and solve their problems. They provide a helpful framework for responding to children as young as three who become unhappy with having downtime.

1. **Lead with sincere empathy.** This may sound like, "Oh, this is really sad. You want me to play with you right now, but I have other things I need to do."
2. **Hand the problem back.** This is achieved by asking, "What do you think you are going to do?"
3. **Ask if they are interested in hearing some ideas.** You might say, "Would you like to hear what some kids decide to do when they feel bored?"
4. **Give them two or three ideas and help them evaluate each.** Examples include:

    - "Some kids decide to color with crayons. How will that work for you?"
    - "Some kids decide to dust the baseboards. How will that work for you?"
    - "Other kids decide to play in the sandbox. How will that work for you?"

Please remember that it is not your job to solve the problem by convincing them to do what you have suggested. Your role is simply to give them options and allow them to learn by deciding whether to choose one of them or do something different.

5. **Allow them to learn from their choice.** Like adults, sometimes children make good choices and sometimes they make poor ones. Because you as a parent are keeping a watchful eye on the situation, the consequences your child may experience from making poor ones will be small yet instructional.

   It's not unusual for younger children to throw tantrums or act out in other ways in response to boredom, especially at first. This is why we are wise to display as few emotions and words as possible. We might simply sing, "Uh-oh," and allow them to spend some quiet time in their playpen, room, or other safe spot. The best consequence for misbehaving when bored is experiencing more boredom.

Step 4. When you see that your child is entertaining themselves, notice and describe what they are doing. Examples include:

"You built that by yourself?"
"That book looks really interesting."
"It looks like you are having a great time playing on the swing."
"I noticed that you made three pictures."
"You decided to get a jump start on the school project that's due next week."

One final point: As we've discussed in previous chapters, the most effective parenting comes by modeling the behavior we want to see in our children. Character and faith are modeled when our children see us demonstrating the strength to tolerate periods of downtime in our own lives. What might happen if we spent less time checking our phones or scrolling through social media and more time interacting with those we love, reading God's Word, or simply being still in prayer and meditation?

I understand this because I have lived it. My PhD in child psychology didn't make parenting easy, and it didn't keep me from occasionally parenting in less-than-optimal ways. Still, allowing plenty of time for supervised outdoor activity, arranging playdates, and providing books and simple but interesting toys are perhaps more important than ever. See the sidebar "The Boredom Training Session" on pages 203–205 for a plan that will help you gradually teach your young child how to entertain themselves while preventing them from becoming addicted to any form of entertainment, including the digital type.

AGE SIX AND BEYOND

Beginning at about age six, our children can gradually begin to have more experience with technology and digital media so they can learn how to have a healthy relationship with it. Please bear with me as I emphasize this: *The primary purpose of giving them tightly limited access starting around age six is for them to develop the attitudes and skills required to relate to this technology wisely.*

The purpose of giving them access is *not* to make them feel loved, to experience social connectedness and acceptance, to gain a sense of freedom, to see themselves as capable, or to meet any other need. We want to see their needs fulfilled, but it's extremely important that our kids learn to get those needs met without digital media before we allow them to have more access to screens.

You might be wondering: *At what age should my kids have their own personal phones, tablets, or other devices they can use anytime they want? When should they be allowed to use social media without supervision?* I can't offer a one-size-fits-all answer, though based on what I've observed, I recommend they not have their own personal devices until they are at least fifteen years of age. Of course, your decision should depend on their level of maturity as demonstrated by the overall quality of their mental health, decision-making, and personal responsibility. The same goes for social media.

To be clear, this does not mean that kids under age fifteen can never use phones or other devices connected to the internet. We can begin to allow elementary-school-aged children very limited access under close supervision. They can do school assignments using these devices when you, or some other trusted adult, are in the room. They should not be allowed to sequester themselves in their rooms under the pretext that they are "doing their homework." School assignments can be completed at the dinner table or in some other common area where you can more easily walk by and see what they are doing. During these ages, you can also begin to occasionally enjoy healthy, God-honoring online information and entertainment *alongside* your children. Very importantly, you are setting limits, allowing them to have no more time spent in front of screens than they actually need for completing schoolwork, scheduling with coaches, and spending a little time enjoying wholesome entertainment under your supervision. Through all of this, it is essential to engage in healthy discussions with your kids about what they are interacting with online.

Again, I advise that kids not participate in social media before age fifteen. This may sound old-fashioned, but it is clear that the risks of doing so far outweigh the benefits. These risks include higher rates of anxiety and depression, elevated rates of suicidal thoughts and feelings, exposure to cyberbullying and other abusive behavior, higher rates of in-person bullying and victimization, elevated risk for screen addiction, exposure to sexualized and violent content, poorer sleep, impaired ability to focus on schoolwork and other important tasks, body image problems, poorer physical fitness, conflict with parents, and more.[5] As you pray about what you have just read, I ask that you carefully consider how difficult it is for many *adults* to use social media in healthy ways. Given this, why would we willingly allow our children, who are just beginning the lifelong process of emotional and spiritual maturation, to be exposed to it?

Well into your child's adolescence, continue to proceed with caution. Don't hesitate to hesitate. Research clearly shows that the longer parents wait to give their kids smartphones, the healthier their children will be. A 2023 global study of 27,969 young adults between the ages of eighteen and twenty-four revealed the following dramatic findings:

- The older a person is when they owned their first smartphone or tablet, the better their mental well-being, and this correlation is stronger in females than males. The percentage of females who experienced mental health challenges dropped from 74 percent in those who received their first smartphone at age six to 46 percent for those who first owned a smartphone at age eighteen. Among males, the percentage of those with mental health issues was 42 percent for those who received their first smartphone at age six and 36 percent for those who first got a phone at age eighteen.
- The aggregate measure of how participants viewed themselves and related to others, which this study refers to as the Social Self, improved most dramatically among both females and males who were older when they first owned a smartphone.
- The prevalence of suicidal thoughts, aggressive feelings toward other people, a sense of detachment from reality, and hallucinations was much lower in those who owned their first smartphone at an older age.[6]

Requiring young people to wait until age fifteen, or even later, to use social media or have their own devices probably seems unrealistic, overly rigid, and unnecessary to some parents. Others may agree with the wisdom of doing so but fear they will be seen by their kids, or even other adults, as being unreasonable or paranoid. Still others worry that saying no will lead to rebellion in their kids. If you are struggling with this decision, remember that it's always easier to give our kids a privilege they have not yet had than to remove one they have grown accustomed to. I have never met a parent who has regretted waiting longer. I have met thousands who deeply regret not doing so.

I also understand that you may have received your first cell phone before age fifteen. As a result, you may disagree with my stance on this topic. After all, you turned out just fine. Or maybe you agree with me because you believe your own childhood would have been far less complicated by toxic images, ideas, and drama if your parents had waited. Wherever you fall, please know that I'm not writing in judgment of your parents or anyone else. We are all scrambling to keep up with technology and its physical, social, emotional, and spiritual impacts. Regardless of what you ultimately decide about the best age to allow your kids to have their own devices and to use social media, it's important to have a strategy for effectively leading them toward developing healthy relationships with these technologies.

So how do you create a plan to effectively help your kids develop healthy relationships with digital devices and the variety of media they support? Because of the ever-changing nature of the technological landscape, we are best served by applying timeless biblical principles, remembering that our Lord never changes and is always more powerful than any new and unforeseen challenges we face. When we do our best to raise children who also believe this, we are giving them the best chance of success in today's fast-paced and unpredictable world.

What About Video Games?

Smartphones may be at the top of most parents' minds when it comes to technology, but video games aren't far behind. Given their popularity, that isn't surprising. About 190 million Americans played video games in 2023; that is millions more than the approximately 183 million Americans who reported reading at least one book that year.[7]

Limited playing of offline games may be appropriate, but only for kids older than six and only after you consider the following questions:

Is the content of the game God-honoring? If you want your children to grow spiritually, as well as socially, emotionally, and behaviorally, you should not do anything that facilitates involvement in activities that glorify sin. This includes video games containing sexualized content, profanity, or immoral and illegal activities such as violence, murder, theft, and the like. The apostle Peter so aptly reminds, "For the Scriptures say, 'You must be holy because I am holy'" (1 Peter 1:16, NLT).

How do you know whether a game's content is appropriate? The only sure way is to preview it. Until you've had a chance to see that it is okay, you are wise to wait before allowing your kids to play it.

Am I willing to limit my child's playing to no more than three hours per week? Why such a conservative time limit? Even simple puzzle or strategy games with healthy content can become extremely addictive. In fact, the most popular ones are built on the same principles that govern the addictive nature of compulsive gambling: Players never know how many more bets they will have to make—or how much longer they will need to play—before they hit something big and exciting. A good hint that our kids are becoming addicted is when we constantly hear them say, "Just give me another minute! I'm almost done!"

My rationale for providing a tight time limit also comes from what I see as dramatically growing numbers of both children and adults who have little tolerance for stillness and quiet. From a spiritual perspective, we know that God does not always speak in loud or dramatic ways. He often does so in a gentle whisper (see 1 Kings 19:11-13). How much of His guidance, correction, and comfort do your kids miss when they are constantly entertained and stimulated?

How is my child responding? Quite frankly, you don't always know how something will work until you try it. This is why it is so important to keep an eye out for symptoms suggesting that you need to enforce tighter limits. Listed below are nine signs to watch for:

- increased irritability, anger, or sadness
- withdrawal
- difficulty concentrating on less stimulating tasks
- more frequent arguing or defiance, particularly around limits you set over game playing
- loss of interest in doing anything other than playing video games
- lack of effort in academics
- increased tiredness
- poor physical fitness
- problems in peer and sibling relationships

If your kids show signs of dependency on video games, it's important that you address it in a calm but deliberate manner. That may include setting much tighter limits on where, how long, and whether your kids are permitted to play on these devices. If they refuse to accept your limits, it may be time to enlist the help of a professional Christian counselor who is experienced in helping families address these issues. (See pages 220–221 for more on this topic.)

Finally, I want to end with what I consider a critically important guideline around video game usage: Do not allow online multiplayer games in your home. Do your best to also help your children ages six and older to understand the risks of these games, including addiction, bullying, exploitation by adults, identity theft, and exposure to malware. Keep your eyes wide open to the fact that predators can easily use chat features in these games to groom kids, luring them into engaging in inappropriate conversations and even meeting in person. Discussing these issues in a factual and unemotional manner will not traumatize your children. It will increase the odds that they will understand why you say no to such games and why they should, too, when they are outside of your home.

FOUR PRINCIPLES TO HELP KIDS DEVELOP A HEALTHY RELATIONSHIP WITH TECHNOLOGY

Principle #1: Healthy Relationships Crowd Out Unhealthy Ones

Our best efforts at self-improvement cannot save us from evil. Garret illustrated this principle for his nine-year-old daughter, Ella. After washing a sink of dirty pots and pans, he invited her to watch something. "Honey, see this empty glass?" he asked. "Look what happens when I cover the top and put it under this nasty water. The inside still looks clean."

A bit confused, Ella replied, "Uh, yeah. What are you doing, Daddy?"

"It takes a lot of work to keep my hand over the opening," he said. "Now notice what happens when I take it off."

As dirty water rushed into the glass, Ella said, "Well, now it's all nasty inside."

"That's what happens," said Garret, "when we try to keep our hearts clean without inviting Jesus to live inside. We aren't strong enough to keep bad stuff from rushing in."

As I noted earlier, children who have good relationships with their parents are far less likely to try to self-medicate through drugs and alcohol, sex, eating disorders, unhealthy technology use, and other destructive behaviors. It is my firm conviction that through His common grace, God provides us an opportunity to give our children a taste of the fullness they can experience only in a relationship with Jesus Christ. It is through our relationship with them, albeit imperfect, that we best point them to the only One who is perfect.

Believe it or not, even when they become teens, our kids want and need plenty of time to connect with their parents, though they may consider it very uncool to admit. Healthy parents don't take this personally, and they don't withdraw when it seems that their kids don't want them around.

Some parents are unable to spend as much time with their families as they wish because they must work long hours, travel for work, or serve in the armed forces. If that describes your situation, you may wonder if this means that you cannot have a powerful, positive impact on your children. Not at all. When kids know their parents yearn to be with them—even though practical considerations sometimes make this impossible—the impact of separation is lessened. A young woman put it this way: "I always knew that my dad wanted to be with me. He constantly left us little notes, sent us letters, called whenever he could, and did everything possible to let us know we were important to him. We always knew that if he had a choice, he would be at home hanging out with us. That really made a difference."

> Even when they become teens, our kids want and need plenty of time to connect with their parents, though they may consider it very uncool to admit.

The main point to remember is simple: Nothing will work without relationships. When our kids have strong and healthy relationships with us, they are also more likely to be equipped with three things that will help them use social media responsibly when they become older teens or adults. The first is the understanding that God loves and values them so much that He gave His only Son to redeem them from their sins. Although faith is clearly a gift from God, and it is not within your power to give it to your children, your love will surely reinforce the fact that God adores them immensely. They are then far less likely to obsessively look for validation from others.

Second, our relationship with our kids gives them a template for relationships with others. The less drama and the more sincere love and respect in our relationships with our kids, the less likely they will subconsciously gravitate toward drama and conflict in peer relationships and interactions with others on social media.

Third, when our children feel bonded with us, they are far more likely to seek and accept our help if they run into trouble. Earlier in this chapter, I shared the story of a father and son who worked through the young man's problem after he viewed pornography and was threatened with blackmail. That's an example of how a close relationship between child and parent can be lifesaving. Obviously, social media presents a variety of potentially serious hazards, some of which are not the user's fault. Cyberbullying and other forms of victimization are widespread. All of us need help, and all of us need to feel safe asking for it.

Principle #2: Relationships Empower Limits and Are Protected by Them

It is interesting to note that the first four of the Ten Commandments center on how we should relate to God. The next six continue this theme yet extend it to the way we should relate to others. These limits are powerful not in and of themselves but within the context of a love relationship with God. We desire to obey Him not only out of a healthy fear of consequences but also out of thankfulness for the grace He has shown us.

In the context of an authentic love relationship with their kids, I encourage parents to use the following relationship-empowered and relationship-protecting limit as the bedrock of their approach to managing their children's technology use:

I provide access to technology only as long as it does not damage our relationship or your relationship with anyone else.

This single limit covers practically unlimited territory. Its broad utility becomes clear when you consider some questions:

- When your kids argue or complain about the rules you provide over technology, is this helping or hurting relationships?

- What rules are important for maintaining healthy relationships with your kids? For example:
  - » No computers or other devices in bedrooms.
  - » No devices during meals.
  - » No devices during church services (except to view the Bible).
  - » No devices when others are trying to have a conversation with you.
  - » Always communicate to others that they are more important to you than a device.
  - » No use of social media until you and your parents agree you are ready.
  - » Do nothing on a device that does not benefit others and bring glory to God.
- When your kids get sneaky by using technology or social media without first asking for permission, is this helping or hurting relationships?
- When your kids use technology or social media in ways that are harmful to themselves or others, does that help or hurt relationships?
- When your kids begin acting bored, unhappy, disengaged, or disrespectful when not allowed to use technology or social media, is that a sign that using it is helping or hurting their relationships?

As we consider how people often respond poorly to God's loving limits, should it surprise us if our kids occasionally argue, complain, and test ours? As a parent I often find it comforting to remember that the more a child protests a limit, the more likely they need it. One parent put it well: "The more my kids argue when I say no, the more practice they need seeing that I love them enough to mean it."

Principle #3: Relationships Require Attention

Keeping a close and loving eye on our kids is one of the most important things we can do to demonstrate our love for them and help them thrive in this digital age. As I noted previously, they may *act* like they don't want connection with us, but they actually crave it. As a young psychologist working with troubled teens, I noticed a recurring theme: They would often do things like shoplift, come home drunk, or leave drugs and drug paraphernalia visible in their rooms. During a session with one of my supervisors, I asked, "Don't they know they are going to get caught? I mean, it's almost as if they want to."

My supervisor, an older and experienced counselor, replied, "That's often why they do it. Many of these kids are wondering, *How out of control do I have to get before my parents see that I need some help? How bad does this have to get before they love me enough to set some limits? When will someone older and wiser than me give me some guidance?*

Far too many parents avoid supervising their kids' digital lives either because they don't want to believe that their children might make poor decisions or because they've been convinced that minors have a constitutional right to privacy. As parents, we do have the right and the responsibility to know what our children and teens are doing. We must do our best to know what devices and apps they are using, along with their passwords. We need to do our best to be aware of their emails and texts, the pictures they keep, and their internet histories.

Caution! This will definitely result in rebellion and sneakiness if we do so with an unloving or overly suspicious attitude. It will backfire if our relationship with our child hasn't been loving, if they have felt ignored, or if our primary focus has been on their weaknesses rather than their strengths. For any chance of success employing these principles, we must do everything we can to create a foundation of mutual love and respect. In love, we must share our concerns about their safety and encourage them to see that we can only help them if they are willing to live within the limits we set. Here's how a parent might open this subject with their teen:

Mom: Why do you think we are so concerned about knowing what you are doing with your devices and online?
Daughter: You don't trust me. I don't know why. Have I ever done anything so horrible?
Mom: I love you, and I don't want you to feel that way. This is mostly about the fact that there is a lot of bullying and other very dangerous things happening online. There are a lot of adults out there who will take advantage of young people if they have an opportunity.
Daughter: You are way too overprotective. I can handle this.
Mom: I believe that you can handle a lot, but all of us need someone to watch over us and help us when we need it. That's why I need to be able to see what is happening on your phone and other devices.

You might imagine the teen then saying, "I don't have to let you know what I am doing."

How might you respond to this? One option is to reply, "I suppose that you could keep things a secret from me, but how would I know that you needed help if something bad was happening?" You might then end the conversation until both of you have calmed down and had time to think.

What if your teen pays for their own device or monthly service? I believe a similar response probably stands the best chance of success. Practically speaking, you and I cannot control whether our teens share their lives with us. Getting into unwinnable control battles serves no benefit either. What we can control is the way we communicate to them that our heart's desire is to help—not to control every move they make. Like so many other scenarios described in this book, this one illustrates our deep dependence on God. He is in control. We are not. Our prayer is that He would protect our kids while also allowing them to grow from the suffering created by their own decisions.

The truth is that it's impossible for us to know everything our kids are doing. Most of us did plenty of things growing up that our parents still don't know about. Yet we *seek* to provide good supervision *not* because we have an infantile belief that we can know everything our kids are doing. We do so *to show them that we care enough to pay attention.* We want to have our eyes wide open to any indicators that they need help.

As I've been alluding to, if we typically operate like consultant parents, rather than hovering helicopters or overcontrolling drill sergeants, the odds are they will be less likely to be deceptive. If we discipline them out of love rather than wrath, the odds are that they will be open and honest rather than secretive and manipulative. On the other hand, if we try to use guilt trips, lecturing, yelling, hovering, micromanaging, or pain, it is true that they will likely grow more deceptive over time.

One more point: When dealing with issues like addiction, repeated legal offenses, or mental health crises, micromanagement is often the best course of action. If you saw your best friend about to walk in front of a bus, would you quietly suggest they move, or would you scream at them and yank them back onto the sidewalk? Micromanagement is bad only when it's the only meal on the menu. In small amounts when the stakes are high, it can be lifesaving.

Principle #4: Relationships Grow Through Accountability

Josh's mother, Wendy, noticed that he seemed completely addicted to his cell phone. If he wasn't connecting with others via social media, he was scrolling through videos or playing yet another mindless online game. Like a genuine addict, he became extremely angry any time she asked him to take a break from it. He was sleeping only a few hours a night, his grades were dropping, and he was even refusing to put the phone away during church.

Josh was fourteen. Wendy had allowed herself to get guilted into giving him a phone a year earlier, and she now realized that it had been a big mistake. Visiting with me after one of my conferences, she told me, "I wish I would have been strong enough to really say no to that phone. I've tried so many times to get him to live within reasonable limits. I've tried rewards, spending more time with him, and even enforcing brief times when he was expected to keep it off. Nothing works. He either ignores me, gets sneaky, or blows up in anger. The thought of really taking it away leaves me feeling guilty because it seems like all his friends have them. I worry that he will hate me if I do that."

After allowing her to express her pain, I replied, "It sounds like you've really tried to be fair and have done a variety of things to help him learn how to keep his phone and use it in responsible ways."

"Yes," she answered, "but he won't settle for anything less than using it almost all the time without following any rules."

"I can't imagine how tough this must be for you," I empathized. "You are not alone. I talk with parents almost every day who say similar things. Would you like my opinion?"

Nodding, she answered, "Yes, I'm stuck. I have no idea where to go from here."

"Maybe it will help if we can think about this in terms of two possible courses of action," I said. "One would be to continue doing what you have been doing. Honestly, I'm fairly certain that this would feed his addiction and create even more conflict between the two of you."

She interrupted. "It's not working. That would be like doing nothing! You are right about him being addicted to it, and our lives are becoming more of a mess every day! He is failing several classes, he looks and sounds exhausted and depressed, and he won't allow me to help in any way."

"Another option," I said, "is to find a good Christian professional who understands how to help young people and their families deal with these types of problems. This person could help you develop a plan to hold him accountable and help him heal from his hurtful, self-destructive behavior."

"What does that mean?" she asked.

Sensing that she needed a very blunt answer, I replied, "After you have made a plan and have support from a professional, the first step would be taking away his phone and any other devices. He won't be able to get them back until he is older and has learned healthier ways of coping with anger, anxiety, boredom, and the other tough feelings that real life and relationships come with."

"But he needs the phone for school and to communicate with his coach." She sighed. "I can't imagine how I could do that."

Before we continue with Wendy's story, I'd like to emphasize three things: First, her story represents an extremely common and complex problem faced by parents. Second, I've seen many success stories, where parents like her have taken the tough steps required to help their kids discover that a life filled with contentment and joy comes only through authentic face-to-face relationships and seeking fulfillment in the only true God rather than the substitutes this world offers. Third, this journey is too complicated and dangerous to take alone. This is why my standard recommendation is that parents find a solid Christian mental health professional who can help them develop a plan *before* they begin to implement it.

Continuing my conversation with Wendy, I shared, "I don't recommend doing anything drastic until you have continued to pray about it and have found a good Christian counselor who can help you develop a plan."

Curious, she asked, "Are you saying that it's okay not to jump into anything until I have a plan?"

"Yes," I answered. "It's essential that you spend time with a professional talking about how you can do this in a safe way that shows your son you love him while also demonstrating that you are not going to back down. The biggest mistakes people make are either never making changes or making them before they've taken the time to choose effective ones they won't come to regret."

"I still worry that my son will hate me for taking his devices!" she exclaimed.

"I think he might in the short term," I agreed. "Either way he's going to be extremely angry with you. But if you prove to him that you love him enough to seek help and to hold him accountable, what are the chances that he will eventually grow into a good man?"

"I don't know," she said, "but I guess that's the only hope I have."

Five years after meeting Wendy, she sent me an email describing how she had chosen hope. The path of working with a Christian counselor had been painful, but it prepared her for the greater difficulty of holding Josh accountable by taking his phone and other devices. After over a year of using technology only under supervision to complete school assignments, he admitted that he felt better. The friendships he was developing were real friendships, and the time he spent with others was real time. On his nineteenth birthday, he shared something that brought tears to her eyes: "Now I realize that when you took my phone away, and wouldn't let me play video games, you saved my life."

Almost daily we as parents must hold our children accountable. Most of the time the issues are small: They have refused to eat their breakfast, they have thrown a tantrum in the store, or they have forgotten to take out the trash. Other times the issues are larger, like the one Wendy faced. We can either let our kids experience our loving discipline or allow the world to eventually teach them in not so loving ways.

To hold them accountable is an act of faith, a belief that something much better will come from doing hard things now. After all, we can trust that God is always true to His promises. "For the moment all discipline seems painful rather than pleasant, but later it yields the peaceful fruit of righteousness to those who have been trained by it" (Hebrews 12:11).

The only path toward raising spiritually strong children is to bring them up in the training and instruction of the Lord. When it comes to technology, that means helping our kids learn to master it before it enslaves them. But as we'll see in the final chapter, we have a role in helping our kids own their faith at every age and stage of their lives.

CHAPTER 10

GOOD EXAMPLES AND RIGHT THINKING

Training Kids to Use God's Truth to Direct Their Lives

"Why didn't you just tell your teacher the truth?" Eloise calmly asked her daughter.

Sobbing, ten-year-old Zoe replied, "I didn't want to do it, but Carmen said that she wouldn't be my friend if I didn't let her copy off my paper."

"Are you saying you felt pressured into letting Carmen see your answers on the quiz, and you didn't tell the truth because you were afraid she wouldn't be your friend?" Eloise asked softly.

Wiping tears from her eyes, Zoe nodded. "Yeah. Then afterward I was afraid I'd get in trouble and God would be mad at me for being so bad."

"I bet this hurts," Eloise continued. "It's hard when you want someone to like you, and they make you feel like you have to do something wrong to make that happen."

"So I'm not in trouble?" Zoe replied with a hint of hope in her voice.

Still speaking with empathy, Eloise replied, "The sad thing is that you still have to face the consequences."

Through renewed tears, Zoe said, "I got a zero on the quiz, and the principal said I don't get to go on the field trip next week. Daddy said that I have to help him do extra chores this weekend because he spent so much time having to talk to Mrs. King about this."

"That is sad," Eloise agreed, hugging her daughter. "Those are a lot of consequences. I hope you know that this doesn't change the way we or God feels about you. All of us make mistakes and must live with the consequences. This is how we learn. The good news is that Jesus died on the cross so that we could be forgiven. That's how much He loves you."

"God isn't mad at me?" Zoe asked.

Eloise answered, "He knows everything about us and still loves us more than we can imagine. The more we trust that this is true, the more we want to do what He says is right."

In this difficult conversation, Eloise was seeking to establish a strong connection with her child while modeling Christ. This meant responding with compassion even after her daughter made a poor decision and had to face the consequences. As we've seen, this is the best way to teach our kids to adopt godly virtues and become spiritually strong, whether they're neglecting their chores or homework, avoiding coming up with solutions to their own problems, or spending too much time watching TV or playing video games.

> The process of learning to lean on His ways is rarely smooth and steady. Each child's path is different and full of twists, turns, peaks, and valleys.

One question remains: How do we actually teach them the true principles of the gospel? How do we prepare our kids to take greater personal responsibility for their own spiritual growth by using God's truth as a plumb line to evaluate their thinking?

In this final chapter, I want to share practical strategies for helping children of all ages learn to use His truth as the standard by which they choose to live their lives. As with the other principles laid out in this book, the process of learning to lean on His ways is rarely smooth and steady. Each child's path is different and full of twists, turns, peaks, and valleys. Every child will need tremendous amounts of our loving patience as they learn about the loving patience of Christ.

AGES AND STAGES: HOW TO BOLSTER KIDS' SPIRITUAL STRENGTH

Before Birth

My strong and unwavering conviction is that children begin learning while still in the womb. Why? In the Psalms, David reflects on God's involvement even before our birth:

> You formed my inward parts;
> you knitted me together in my mother's womb.
> I praise you, for I am fearfully and wonderfully made.
> **PSALM 139:13-14**

Research has consistently documented the staggering amount of brain development in utero: "To arrive at the more than 100 billion neurons that are the normal complement of a newborn baby, the brain must grow at the rate of about 250,000 nerve cells per minute, on average, throughout the course of pregnancy."[1]

There is also no doubt that the experiences of the expectant mother affect her unborn child, greatly impacting the development of neurological connections and structures. Generally speaking, the safer and the more loved and supported the mother feels, the more likely the child's brain will have an early opportunity to begin the long process of healthy maturation.[2]

Since fathers play a key role in providing stability for expectant moms, both parents play a huge role. Those of us who are fathers can either act in supportive ways that bless our wives, or we can make things harder for them. I heard one dad put it like this: "Ephesians 5:25 says, 'Husbands, love your wives, as Christ loved the church and gave himself up for her.' Doing this is one way that I can start showing my kids the love of God even before they are born."

This is also the ideal time for parents to start habits they will continue throughout their children's lives: praying with their children, reading Scripture to them, and sharing stories of God's love and faithfulness. Just because preborn babies are unable to converse doesn't mean they can't benefit from these conversations. The reasons for this go far beyond what research on prenatal brain development reveals. God works in supernatural, often unmeasurable ways to bless and strengthen those who love Him. When we take the leap of faith required to believe that He is working on our children's minds while they are still in the womb, we please Him greatly.

In Infancy

The greatest blessing and challenge of parenting infants is their complete dependency. Unless their needs are consistently attended to, they will not survive. God designed it this way for a perfect reason: Parents can give their children a picture of His loving provision. This foundation is crucial for the development of trust and spiritual strength.

In chapter 3, we looked at the trust cycle. Children learn to trust whenever their parents respond to their cries and meet their needs. They learn they are loved apart from anything they can do in return. Likewise, we come to faith in Jesus Christ as we see Him love and care for us despite the fact that we can do nothing to earn His love. The faith of children who don't feel such unconditional love, on the other hand, may be stunted by anxiety, fear, and defensiveness.

The Toddler to Preschool Years

Young children remain deeply dependent upon us for their needs, but they are also developing a strong desire for independence and the ability to exercise it. As always, God's plan is perfect, as this period provides a wonderful opportunity for parents to start doing two additional things that have a strong impact on the development of spiritual strength:

- apply the Three E's of Growth;
- introduce the basic idea that everyone—including God—has thoughts.

The Three E's of Growth

In chapter 4, we considered the meaning of discipline when it comes to forming our children's character. Essentially, we are wise to consistently do three things to promote emotional health, positive behavior, and spiritual growth in our kids. I call these three things "The Three E's of Growth": providing a good *example*, allowing our children to learn from *experience*, and holding them accountable for their actions with *empathy* rather than anger or shame.

The connection between these three E's and spiritual growth is a powerful one. Faith is heavily impacted by seeing the *example* of others. One of the most important ways that children develop the ability to align their thinking with God's truth is by watching their parents grow in this way.

Memorable examples abound in Scripture, too, so another extremely powerful way to help our children learn is by reading them stories of courage through faith. Notable examples include Noah and the ark, David and Goliath, Daniel and the lions' den, and the Israelites marching and blowing their trumpets until the walls of Jericho tumbled down. Stories stick in our minds and parables penetrate our hearts in amazing ways. (That's why a bonus of reading stories such as these to our children is the impact they have on our *own* faith.)

Young children also benefit from hearing our personal stories of faith and courage, as well as those shared by their grandparents and other adults they love. This is one of the values of keeping a prayer journal. If you haven't done this yet, start by doing your best to recall the trials you have faced and how God helped you get through them. Begin to record how your prayers are being answered by God. Also try to recall how God has answered the prayers of others you know and then write down those experiences. As time goes by, you will have a wealth of stories of God's faithfulness to share with your children, and someday, your children's children.

There is no substitute for personal *experience* in the development of faith. This is why kids need to experience the connections and joy that service brings. There is no need to wait until your children are older to begin involving them. In fact, failing to involve them represents a massive lost opportunity. Whether it is having your child write a letter to a child your family sponsors through a nonprofit like Compassion or World Vision or helping you carry dinner to an elderly widow on your block, faithful thinking and faithful works build upon each other. Without each, faith remains stunted.

As much as we might wish that our kids learned only from positive experiences, our children's faith also grows as a result of them testing our limits. As crazy as this sounds, it is true! When it comes to developing a trust cycle toward Christ, don't forget the three stages in which parents play a key role by establishing loving limits. The child thinks:

- *I don't get to do or have everything that I want.*
- *It's okay to submit to a loving person who is bigger and stronger than I am.*
- *I am still loved even when I make mistakes.*

Because kids can test limits only if they have them, and they learn to develop healthy beliefs about trust by doing so, it's essential that parents begin to set *empathetic* yet firm limits as soon as their children are old enough to spit out pureed sweet potatoes, grab items they shouldn't touch, or experiment with any other undesirable behavior.

Most experts in child development agree that a person's most foundational beliefs are largely developed by ages three to four, and they are learned primarily through example, experience, and empathy.

Introducing the Power of Thoughts

Around this time, parents can also help their children begin to understand the abstract notions of thinking and believing: You have thoughts, I have thoughts, and God has thoughts. This can be done by playing a simple game I call Guess What I Am Thinking.

Four-year-old Hannah was excited when her daddy, James, scooped her up in his arms and said, "Let's play a game, honey!"

"What?" she squealed with joy.

"It's called Guess What I Am Thinking."

Clearly confused, Hannah replied with a stare. "What is it?"

"When people think things," said James, "they say something to themselves without talking. I'll show you. Watch me." He raised his eyebrows and smiled broadly.

Even more confused, Hannah said, "Your face looks funny, but you didn't say anything!"

"That's because I am thinking about something that makes me laugh. I was thinking about the clown we saw at Adam's birthday party."

"Yeah," Hannah said, giggling, "that clown was silly!"

"Now you think of something," continued James, "and I will try to guess what you are thinking."

"Okay, look at me!" Hannah ordered with a laugh.

"I think you are also thinking about that clown," James replied.

Hanna answered, "No. I was thinking about Adam when he got cake on his face."

Playing this sweet and simple game can help children gradually develop a greater awareness that thinking is a real and important part of everyone's lives. As they begin to better understand this concept, it's helpful to begin expanding to brief discussions about God and His thoughts.

"Let's go on a walk, Hannah," James said.

"Where are we going?" Hannah questioned.

"I see some flowers out in the yard. Let's go look," he replied.

Stopping before their rosebushes, Hannah pointed to a bud. "This one is yellow!" Hannah exclaimed.

"Yes! That is yellow," James answered. "There are a lot of other things out here. Look at the sky. It's blue. Look at Cruiser, our dog; he is brown and has white paws. Look at the grass. It's green. What do you think God thinks about all of this?"

"Who is God?" Hannah asked.

"God is the One who made us and everything in the world," James replied. "He looks at everything He made and thinks, *This is good!*"

"He must be really tired," Hannah said. "That's a lot of things to make."

Laughing, James answered, "No, He never gets tired. He is so strong that He can do anything."

"He must be big!" Hannah replied.

"Yep! God is big, and He has a lot of thoughts that are big and important too. I brought the Bible with me so that I can read to you more about what He thinks."

"You and Mommy read that book a lot! Is it a story?" Hannah asked.

"Yes!" James said. "It's full of what God thinks. It can help us learn to think more like Him."

Kindergarten Through the Early Elementary School Years

By now you likely understand that one of your responsibilities as a parent is to help your children learn that the quality of their thinking affects the quality of their lives. When parents start very early, their children are well on their way toward developing this understanding by the time they reach the age of five. During this next stage, parents can begin to help kids learn to assess their own thoughts even as they learn to apply God's truth.

Thinking About Thoughts

Around this age, parents can also begin to help their kids understand that people evaluate their thinking in one of two ways. Some use their own thoughts and feelings to determine what is true. Others use God's Word. Popular culture tells our kids that they ought to determine the accuracy of their thoughts by trusting their hearts. As Christians, we know that this is a horrible idea: "The heart is deceitful above all things, and desperately sick; who can understand it?" (Jeremiah 17:9).

The practice of trusting one's personal feelings as truth reflects the foundational principle of relativism: There is no such thing as objective truth. People get to make it up based on their own feelings or desires. A powerful study of the impact of this ideology can be found in the book of Judges. At this time, societal chaos reigned as "everyone did what was right in his own eyes" (Judges 21:25). Such chaos continues to rule in the lives of those who believe they have the right to make up their own rules.

Personal and societal peace and order can be found only when we place God's ways and His truth above our thoughts and feelings. Because of this, it is essential that we teach our children that the only standard for accurately judging thoughts or ideas, including our own, is the truth found within the pages of the Bible. As children approach kindergarten age, they can begin to grasp the concept that Scripture is God's level and plumb line. This is most fun and effective when we use actual tools to demonstrate it. An inexpensive level is available from most home improvement stores. A simple plumb line can be made by hanging a heavy bolt from a string.

William used these tools to begin a very important conversation with his six-year-old son, Joshua.

One day after dinner, William asked Joshua to follow him to the living room, where he held out a framed photo. Behind him he had already hung a picture hook. "I took this picture of you on your birthday," William said. "Do you remember?"

"Yes!" Joshua replied. "That was at the park."

"Let's put it on the wall right here," William replied, purposely hanging the picture very crookedly.

Joshua's excitement quickly faded. "That looks bad, Dad!" he exclaimed.

Smiling, William replied, "Yes, I think you are right. And just like this picture is crooked, sometimes our thinking isn't quite right either. But what do you think is wrong with the picture?"

"It's leaning. It's gonna fall," Joshua answered with concern. "How do we fix it?"

"We can use these two tools I have right here," William answered as he showed Joshua the small level and the plumb line he had made. "We can use these to make sure that your picture is hanging straight and won't slip off the hook. If we rest this tool, called a level, on the top edge of the picture, we can see which way to move it to make sure that it is straight. We can also hang this line, called a plumb line, against either the left or right edge of the picture. This will also help us see whether the picture is straight. Sometimes people call that being plumb."

As they worked together, this loving father continued: "Do you remember when I told you I was sorry this morning after I honked at the driver ahead of us in the school drop-off line?"

"Yes," said Joshua. "Mrs. Peters was so slow!"

"Well, I got irritated and didn't stop to think. Then I felt bad when I saw her little girl struggling to put on her backpack and carry a big box of cupcakes. I remembered that God tells us in the Bible that love is patient and kind. I sure didn't show that to you or Mrs. Peters.

"Just like the level is helping us get this picture hung straight, God gave us the Bible to help us keep our own thinking and lives straight. When our thoughts match God's, they are plumb and level—or right according to God's ways. This helps keep us from making big mistakes that can hurt us and others."

William also shared how Jesus gave His life so that we can be forgiven. "Son, we always want to do our best to have true and good thoughts because this helps us have true and good behavior. This pleases God, and it makes our lives way better. The good news, though, is that we don't have to be perfect. I sure am not. Nobody is. When you trust Jesus, He forgives you for your mistakes."

These are big ideas for a little person to understand, so parents are wise to take it slow and frequently repeat these fun lessons in different ways.

At about this time, parents can also teach their children why they do not have to be imprisoned by negative, ungodly thoughts or emotions. Each of us is responsible for how we think and feel, and the good news is that trusting Christ sets us free to choose thoughts and beliefs that are true, hopeful, and healthy. One way to teach this is by purposefully allowing our kids to overhear us talking about this concept as it plays out in our lives. This is another way we can apply the first "E" of Growth.

As he drove his family across town to visit some friends, Jose said to his wife, Melinda, "Yesterday, I had a customer really put me down. He was very impatient with me and said some nasty and untrue things."

Q & A: What Might You Do When Your Kids Complain About Going to Church?

At some point practically every child will test to see how truly committed their parents are to their spiritual growth. One way they do this is by grumbling about attending church or threatening that they simply will not go. Sometimes they even act out while there, subconsciously checking to see if they can make the experience unpleasant enough to keep their parents from taking them. However your child expresses displeasure at going to church, here are some ways you might respond:

- **Take them anyway, and don't display any hesitation.** When parents calmly and consistently demonstrate to their children that church attendance is nonnegotiable, kids learn that there's no point in objecting. Of course, this requires that they learn that arguing, complaining, or acting out will not cause us to change our minds.

  Our attitude is also important. They absolutely must see that we desire to attend out of love for Christ and His people, not from some cold, dogmatic sense of obligation.

- **Don't let embarrassment or shame get in the way.** Some children act so poorly in church that their parents feel too embarrassed to return. Please don't let this happen; instead, reach out to the church for help. None of us are perfect, and none of us have perfect kids.

  Just as importantly, remember that allowing your child to use bad behavior to keep you from attending church will only serve to reward their bad behavior. It will also deprive them of opportunities to build positive relationships that will help them learn to fall in love with church and God.

- **Find ways to get them connected through more relationships and opportunities to serve.** Going to a new church can feel a little scary. It can feel overwhelming. It can seem like a lonely place crowded with people. I have also learned that relationships and service can turn this around very quickly. The more time we and our children serve with others at church, the quicker we feel part of the community.

- **Don't make the mistake of trying to find the "perfect" church for you or your kids.** Many parents these days choose a church based on whether or not their kids like the music, find the pastor entertaining, or enjoy the youth group. When these boxes are checked off, they determine it's the place to join. The obvious problem is that often little consideration is given to the following questions:

    - Is the teaching biblically sound?
    - Is it a warm place where people care enough about each other to speak the truth in love?
    - Does it acknowledge that it is imperfect like you, me, and even the most faithful Christians?
    - Is it a place where my family and I can learn that it truly is more blessed to give than to receive?

Well over a century ago, Charles Spurgeon reminded his listeners that imperfect people searching for a perfect church do so in vain: "If I had never joined a church till I had found one that was perfect, I should never have joined one at all; and the moment I did join it, if I had found one, I should have spoiled it, for it would not have been a perfect church after I had become a member of it."[3]

"People can act very mean at times," Melinda empathized.

Jose continued, knowing that their children, Micah and Grace, were most certainly listening carefully from the back seat of the car. "Yes, people can say some hurtful things. When this happens it's easy for me to start thinking mean or hurtful thoughts. This is natural, but it can cause big problems. This is when we are more likely to say or do things that get us in trouble."

"Yes, it is tempting to do that," Melinda agreed. "I struggle with that too. That's why we all need Jesus."

Jose nodded, adding, "I was starting to get really upset, and then I remembered, *Wait! Jesus gives me the strength to choose what I spend my time thinking about. I can either choose to think about things that please Him or things that don't. I don't have to treat people poorly just because they are acting mean.*"

"That's right," Melinda agreed.

"I decided to think about how God tells us to always treat people well, regardless of how they treat us," Jose continued. "I also started thinking about the fact that people who act mean really need someone to show them the love of Jesus. I'm so thankful that God helped me remember this."

"So, did you feel any better?" Melinda asked.

"Yes, but it was still hard," Jose admitted. "The most important thing is that I was able to be kind rather than doing something that I would have regretted."

No person or situation can make us think or feel anything. When we struggle with negative emotions, God is there. When we are tempted by ungodly thoughts, He is right by our side: "The Lord helps the fallen and lifts those bent beneath their loads" (Psalm 145:14, NLT). People who understand this truth are far more resilient physically, emotionally, and spiritually.

A few days later, Melinda walked into the room to see Micah

becoming upset over some homework he was trying to complete. "It looks like you are having a really hard time," she said.

"I'm just stupid. I can't do anything right!" Micah cried.

Gently stroking his hair, Melinda said, "Aren't you glad I don't believe that?"

Micah raised his eyes, tears streaming down his cheeks. "I still think I am," he continued.

Gently and lovingly, Melinda replied, "You are having a hard time with math. That doesn't mean you can't do anything right. When we think and say things about ourselves that aren't true, it's like we are bullying ourselves. God doesn't want that for you. You get to choose what you think and feel."

Micah sobbed. "I don't know."

"Micah," his mother replied, "I can't make you believe one thing or another, but I will pray that you will give some thought to the fact that when we think and say hurtful things to ourselves, we always feel horrible. Fortunately, we can share this with Jesus and ask Him to help us think more positively."

During this conversation, Melinda shared her heart with her son. Doing so, she unwittingly applied the second and third "E's" of Growth: She pointed out that the consequences of Micah's thinking were causing him to *experience* great pain, and she did so with sincere *empathy*. Most importantly, she directed him to God, who is the ultimate source of our comfort and growth.

Scripture Memorization

For each of us to choose God's thoughts, we must know them. By this age, children are also ready to begin building their mental database of Scripture and related spiritual principles. This can only come from time spent learning the actual words of the Bible. The more parents read and explain it to their children, the more likely their kids will have internalized solid spiritual standards by the time they approach adolescence. These standards are the ones that will make the difference when their bodies are filled with hormones and their minds are bombarded with a dizzying number of new and enticing ideas. If children begin filling their hearts with God's Word early on, they will find the huge life challenges starting in adolescence far easier to navigate.

> How can a young man keep his way pure?
> By guarding it according to your word.
> With my whole heart I seek you;
> let me not wander from your commandments!
> I have stored up your word in my heart,
> that I might not sin against you.
>
> **PSALM 119:9-11**

Memorizing Bible verses is a powerful way for them to stamp God's Word on their hearts. It's also an effective way for parents to model the power of His Word. When kids grow accustomed to watching their parents memorize Scripture, the odds are much higher that they will do so also. The depth of understanding is far more important than the number of verses that kids can recite.

If children begin filling their hearts with God's Word early on, they will find the huge life challenges starting in adolescence far easier to navigate.

Years ago, I served in a Bible memorization ministry at our church. Etched in my mind is the face of an extremely sweet seven-year-old as he fired off an impressive list of verses he'd memorized. After encouraging his great effort, I asked him to pick one and tell me what it meant. I don't remember the specific one he chose, but I do remember what it meant to him: "My mom and dad said that if I learn more than five, I get to have a soda when we stop for gas on the way home."

Again, I want to emphasize that there is great value in kids memorizing Scripture if they also seek to understand the underlying truth in each passage. Doing so can play a very significant role in helping them grow in spiritual strength since they'll be able to bring God's truth to mind when they need it most. To model the value of Scripture memorization, experiment with doing the following:

- About twice a month, pick a brief Bible passage to memorize, understand, and apply.
- Seek wise counsel to help you understand what God has intended it to mean and how we are called to apply it.
- With excitement and joy, talk with your kids about what you have learned and let them overhear you talking about this to others.
- Pray that God will give you opportunities to model for your children what it looks like to apply the verse.
- Invite them to participate with you as you memorize and learn to apply what you are discovering.

Young children can begin memorizing a few Bible verses, or segments of verses, as young as age five or six. Listed below are some quick tips:

- **Start with a short prayer, asking God for His help.** You might pray with your child a simple prayer like this: "Dear Lord Jesus, we love You. Please help us remember what we are about to learn."
- **Pick one verse at a time, starting with simple ones.** A good example is "A soft answer turns away wrath, but a harsh word stirs up anger." (Proverbs 15:1).
- **Explain the core meaning of the verse in language your child can understand.** For the verse mentioned above, you might say,

"When we talk softly and say something nice to other people, they are more likely to say something kind to us. We usually get the best treatment from others when we first treat them nicely."

- **With enthusiasm and love, read the verse to them at least once per day.** Repetition over long periods of time is the key to effective learning, particularly with very young children. As we apply this principle, it is also essential to remember that the enthusiasm and love they experience from us will go a long way toward helping them fall in love with learning God's Word.
- **With great love and patience, spend very short periods of time guiding them to recite it back to you.** When your child has heard the verse multiple times, begin to help them repeat it back to you. Avoid spending more than five to ten minutes doing this at a time, and don't display frustration or discouragement if your child doesn't learn it quickly. The main goal is that they have fun and experience your love and patience throughout.
- **Enjoy the process with your kids.** The more relaxed and joyful you can remain as you help your kids learn Scripture, the more likely it is that they will come to associate studying God's Word with positive feelings rather than negative ones. The most important goal at any age is to help our children fall in love with and trust Jesus. I find it helpful to constantly remind myself that salvation is by grace and grace alone. It is not dependent upon our—or our children's—ability to accurately recite Bible verses.

A dad attending one of my conferences shared how studying Proverbs 15:1 with his seven-year-old daughter, Olivia, paid off for both of them. "I prayed to God that I wouldn't just teach her to memorize verses but that I would have the strength to show her how to live them out.

"God answered my prayer in the form of my next-door neighbor constantly complaining about our trash cans being placed too close to his property line," he told me. Unfortunately, he had little control over the issue because the trash collector sometimes put the cans on the neighbor's property line after he dumped their contents into his truck.

"Our neighbor didn't care about that," this man told me. "Every time it happened, he'd run over, knock on the door, and yell at me about it. One day, the garbage truck had barely pulled away, and he was rapping on my door. On the verge of losing my temper, I remembered this verse and replied to him with kindness instead of what I felt like saying. I was glad I did because our seven-year-old, Olivia, happened to walk in the room at that precise moment."

A week or so later, he said, Olivia came home from school and told him how a kid in her class had been picking on her. She continued, "I just said to myself, *A soft answer turns away wrath, but a harsh word stirs up anger.*" When her dad asked her how following that proverb worked for her, she said, "Good, because I didn't get in trouble for fighting back."

Seeking God's Truth in Prayer

Finally, this is the perfect age for parents to begin guiding their children through the "My Prayer for Truth" exercise we discussed in chapter 2 (see page 39). It's a great way to help children discover the power of the truths God has shared in His Word. Consider this example involving a child who is feeling fearful about going to a new school:

MY PRAYER FOR TRUTH

- Dear Lord, I have been feeling *afraid to go to school and sad and bad about myself.*
- I have found myself thinking: *I hate school. I hate those kids. Nobody will ever like me.*

- Lord, what does Your Word teach about this? *You love me, and You say to be kind to people who are mean. What You say about me is true. What the kids who are picking on me are saying isn't. With Your help I can be strong and solve this problem.*
- Lord, please help me dwell on what You say is true and on nothing else. I want my deepest thoughts and beliefs to reflect Your goodness.

Preadolescence and Beyond

This stage in your kid's life is a critical one because at some point they will need to make their faith their own. While it may not feel as natural to talk with them about spiritual matters as it does to discuss other things, it's more important than ever for you to do so. Please do not fall into the trap of believing that your older children and teens will only learn important spiritual truths outside your home. They still benefit from having conversations with you about God and how His Word applies to daily life. They still need to witness your love for and trust in Him. At this age, however, it can also be helpful to encourage them to branch out and grow by learning from other godly people.

There are three steps that are important, though by no means are they the only ways you can encourage your kids to follow Christ:

1. **Encourage kids to seek godly mentors at church and in your community.** As preteens and teens begin to test their independence, they will naturally begin to also look to peers and adults outside your home for direction. When it comes to our children's continuing spiritual development, many Christian families depend on their church's youth group as a place to find that support. In fact, during this often-challenging period, it is essential that adolescents begin to branch out and develop relationships with other kids and

adults who are devoted to building their relationships with Jesus Christ. Through solid Bible teaching, friendships with peers, and mentorship from adult leaders, a youth group can give our kids wonderful opportunities to see that following Jesus is far more fulfilling than giving in to the unhealthy temptations presented by this world.

When evaluating youth groups, keep your eyes wide open to the following:

- *Not all youth groups promote a biblical faith.* Groups that focus exclusively on exciting events and fun activities at the expense of biblical instruction and mentoring don't just miss the mark. They can be damaging because they seek to win youth to Christianity with something other than Christ. The old saying "We win people to what we win them with" applies here. If our kids are enticed by an incomplete, overly glamorized version of the gospel, their faith may not be real or enduring. At the opposite end of the spectrum, groups that demand cold obedience to a very rigid code of thinking and behavior also promote a false gospel.
- *Not all youth groups are healthy.* Many youth group leaders have tremendous gifts and skills for helping kids grow in their faith. They should be encouraged and prayed for often. Some people placed in this position of leadership, however, are not ready for the responsibility or do not possess the necessary gifts and skills. Some even behave in ways that are almost indistinguishable from the teens they serve. The natural result is that the group fails to mature, and very unhealthy, sometimes ungodly behavior within the group goes unnoticed or is allowed or even reinforced.

Q & A: What Might You Do If Your Kids Question the Christian Faith?

Even as you seek to shore up your own faith, you may discover that your kids are wrestling with questions of their own. Sooner or later, bright kids are likely to wonder about the validity of what the Bible teaches, as well as their own personal faith. My prayer is that this happens as early in their lives as possible. Far better that they begin questioning when they are still under your roof and you have time to nurture their character and understanding of Christian apologetics.

When your child brings you their doubts, I recommend you do the following:

- **Don't panic.** Instead, thank them for sharing their questions and opinions. Our children need to see that we are not threatened, angered, or racked with anxiety when they ask questions or even make bold statements, such as "I don't see how any of this can be true." When we remain calm or at least do a good job of acting like we are, we model confidence. We also demonstrate that our love for them is not based on whether they always agree with our values.

  We should be genuinely thankful that our children feel comfortable enough to share their questions and thoughts.

- **Show that you are actively listening as they speak.** In situations like this, ears are more effective than mouths. As they share their hearts, the only time we should use our tongues is when we're asking thoughtful questions to help us better understand their perspective.

- **Before sharing your perspective, ask them if they would like to hear it.** Though this step can be scary for some parents, it's helpful to remember that showing this small bit of respect makes it far more likely that your kids will actually consider what you have to say. Unsolicited opinions and advice are rarely taken to heart.

  At this point many parents find themselves lost for good answers to their kids' objections. Saying, "Well, the Bible is the inspired Word of God. Everything in it is true" may be accurate, but it's unlikely to convince a bright, strong-minded child. Far more effective is saying something like "That is such a great question. Would you be interested in researching this with me?"

If they take you up on this, I recommend books by two authors that you can read together. These resources offer a logical defense of Christianity, and each has a version for kids:

- *Another Gospel?* and *Another Gospel? Student Edition* by speaker and author Alisa Childers
- *The Case for Christ* and *The Case for Christ for Kids* by pastor and author Lee Strobel
- *Cold-Case Christianity* by J. Warner Wallace, cold-case detective, author, and Christian apologist, and *Cold-Case Christianity for Kids* by J. Warner Wallace and Susie Wallace

- **Throughout this process, emphasize that God is the only source of true faith.** Ultimately, faith requires a supernatural act of God. We have it by grace, not because of our own works or those of any other human being. Studying apologetic resources can be extremely helpful, but in itself, it cannot perform spiritual heart transplants. Our children must know this. They must also know that if they earnestly seek God, they will find Him, and He will never leave them, even when they struggle to understand His ways.

- *Youth groups benefit greatly from having male and female leaders of various ages.* There is strength in numbers. A leadership team can pray for one another and hold each other accountable. If one leader begins to head in the wrong direction, others can pull them back. In addition, if a teen doesn't seem to connect with one, they may connect with another. It takes far more than one or two adults to adequately supervise even a small group of teens.

- *Leaving your church for a "better" youth group is a very serious decision.* If you and your kids have a loving and godly church family, it is a precious blessing that God will use to grow you and your kids. Needlessly leaving such a church may result in far more problems than it solves. It is also important to remember that participation in a youth group is not required for social, emotional, or spiritual growth. Learning, serving, and experiencing fellowship with godly people of many ages is the surest way for young people to grow spiritually.

2. **Acknowledge and address hypocrisy.** As adolescence nears, many kids become keenly aware of hypocrisy. This is particularly true when they see it in adults. Because of this, they are primed to learn how to begin assessing and growing in the agreement between their formal beliefs—what they know they *should* believe—and functional beliefs—how they typically behave. Hypocrisy stems from a consistent lack of agreement between the two, particularly when our actions don't match our stated formal beliefs. Authenticity is demonstrated when what we do matches what we say we believe.

   When our kids reach this age, some appropriate self-disclosure by parents to their kids can be helpful. By occasionally sharing examples of how we have failed to live up to the beliefs we profess, our kids see that godly people mourn over the hypocrisy in their own hearts. We can then demonstrate that the only way to combat this is to confess it and seek the grace of God.

An embarrassing example from my own life comes to mind, involving a not-so-gracious interaction I had with someone at the gym. While working out, I noticed that one guy was acting rudely toward some teens who were also trying to use the equipment. These young people were handling it well, but I allowed my prideful desire to be the hero get in the way. Instead of minding my own business, I took it upon myself to lecture the older guy about how he ought to stop being so selfish about sharing the equipment. Immediately afterward, I felt the pain of realizing that I had chosen to combat rudeness with more rudeness. Even more painful was the fact that one of my sons witnessed the event. After praying about this, I concluded that I needed to admit this sin to my son and share with him how I also confessed it to God.

> Some appropriate self-disclosure by parents shows our kids that godly people mourn over the hypocrisy in their own hearts and combat this by confessing it and seeking the grace of God.

"I really blew it yesterday when we were at the gym," I told him.

"What do you mean?" my son asked.

"I was unkind to that guy who wasn't sharing the equipment," I answered.

Clearly surprised, he quipped, "No way. That guy was so inconsiderate. He was hogging everything, and he was griping about those other guys just trying to use it."

"Yes, he was being rude to those guys, but they had it handled," I said. "The problem is that I have always taught you how important it is to treat people graciously. Then I didn't do it myself."

"That's okay, Dad." He smiled and added, "It's not like you were a total jerk. You were just a little bit of a jerk."

"Very funny," I said. "But seriously, God treats us way better than we deserve, so we should do the same for others. I'm praying that He will help me do a better job of remembering this in the future."

Do you see how the Three E's of Growth apply even here? Throughout their lives our children must witness us setting an *example* through our reliance on God to overcome the sin in our own lives. As preteens and adolescents, they test even more limits and push even more buttons to see if we will continue to practice what we preach. Their *experience* with these tests of our true character will have an impact on their lives. When parents respond with *empathy* rather than anger or frustration, we display the love and power of Jesus. It is during the greatest times of trial that we can have the greatest positive impact on their lives.

3. **Show compassion when consequences kick in.** A very godly friend and colleague once approached me with great pain in his eyes. As I remember, he started the conversation by asking, "Can I share something personal with you?" My friend went on to describe how he felt like a huge failure because his seventeen-year-old son had been arrested for underage drinking and driving while under the influence.

   Some people react to stories such as these by thinking, *We're not the kind of family that things like this happen to. There is no drinking in our home, and we have always raised our kids to put God first.* As you certainly know, the godliest of parents can still have children who make big mistakes.

It was clear that my friend was hurting deeply and needed me to listen rather than offer any advice. As I did, he described how his son had always been a conscientious and responsible kid who'd never been in any serious trouble. He also shared how he and his wife were struggling with how to handle the situation. As you might imagine, they were shocked and in disbelief when they received the call from the sheriff's department. Apparently, the only thing they could initially think to say to their son was "We love you, and we are sure that you will find a way to deal with the consequences."

He told me that he and his wife stayed up all night praying and thinking about what they would do. Nothing came to mind except the parable of the prodigal son, the story of the young man who returned home humbled after demanding his father give him his inheritance and then wasting it all. When the son sought forgiveness, his father gave it to him.

This parable offers many powerful lessons, one of which is that God allows us to face the consequences of our rebellion but always offers His forgiveness when we admit that we need it.

After praying long and hard about the problem, my friend and his wife realized that two things were required for their son to learn from this experience. They needed to demonstrate love and forgiveness while also allowing him to experience the full brunt of the consequences for his actions. His life was much harder for quite a while, largely because he was not allowed to drive the family car and had to find a way to pay for all the legal fees and other related costs. He was required by the court to be on probation and complete community service.

Something his father said still sticks in my mind: "At first, we felt a bit guilty for treating him with love and forgiveness. Then it hit us. It's God's love that really helps us learn and become more like Him."

Many years have passed since my friend and his family went through this struggle. He often remarks at what a powerfully positive impact this had on their entire family. "It is true that we ought to consider it pure joy when we face trials. If anything, this crisis helped our relationship become stronger as we emotionally supported our son as he lived through the many problems he'd created for himself. It also helped us show his younger brother and sister what love is all about."

We demonstrate the truest form of love when we reflect God's commandments and His grace. When our thinking is oriented toward loving Him with all that we have *and* loving others as we love ourselves, we serve Him well and show our children how to do so also. As much as we want our children to grow in virtues and character, love for and commitment to God will be at the heart of their spiritual strength. It's also the source of our deepest satisfaction in having led them His way: "I have no greater joy than to hear that my children are walking in the truth" (3 John 1:4).

As you've read this book, I pray that love has stood out as a primary theme. Our ability to experience and share it is made possible only because of God's love for us. From it flows all good things, including the ability to teach our children virtues such as love, respectfulness, humility, obedience, honesty, accountability, contentment, generosity, strength, perseverance, and the wisdom required to successfully navigate temptations and troubles. I pray that through a relationship with Christ, your children will live out these virtues—not as burdensome obligations—but as joyful fruit from the Holy Spirit.

Finally, my dear friend, please remember that you do not have to be perfect. You have a perfect God who is completely loving, completely strong, and completely in control. While raising spiritually strong kids isn't always easy, His power is made perfect in your deepest times of weakness and need. He loves you and your kids more than you can imagine!

ACKNOWLEDGMENTS

There is no doubt that the Lord used many wonderful people to make this book possible.

Without the ever-present support, encouragement, and patience of my wife, Monica, I would have never finished it! For days and days, seemingly without end, you worked hard to pick up the slack in our lives, allowing me to close myself off from just about everything else to write and complete edits. You encouraged me in the times of discouragement that accompany such a task, and I have profited tremendously from your wisdom. "An excellent wife who can find? She is far more precious than jewels" (Proverbs 31:10). You are that "excellent wife," and I love you!

Great gratitude also goes to my father, Jim Fay. Dad, thanks for your love and all that you have taught me. Your development of the Love and Logic approach has helped me so much, and I know that these ideas will also be a blessing to those who read this book!

I'm also extremely thankful for the wisdom of our good friend Foster Cline, MD. Foster, for many decades, you have taught me—and countless others—priceless lessons about raising kids. I will always be thankful for your assistance in helping my dad create the Love and Logic approach.

Much appreciation goes to Daniel Amen, MD. Daniel, thanks so much for your encouragement, wisdom, and support, all of which have made it possible for the Love and Logic approach to continue and grow. You and your work have been a blessing to millions of people.

The team at Tyndale House Publishers has also been a blessing from God:

> Great thanks go to Jan Long Harris. Jan, thanks for encouraging me to write this book and for the direction and great editorial wisdom you have given me.
>
> Thanks also go to Jillian Schlossberg. Jillian, your early editorial insights helped get me on the right track as I began the project.
>
> Great gratitude goes to Kimberly Miller, who served an indispensable role as my primary editor. Kim, without your immense organizational, writing, and editorial gifts, this book would have been a jumbled mess. Yes, God used you to bring clear form to a manuscript that desperately needed it. Your kindness, encouragement, and patience with my limitations have made all the difference.
>
> The gifts and hard work of countless others at Tyndale made this book possible, including those who worked on the layout, cover design, copyediting, and the many other details. Thanks to all of you!

Finally, I thank all who will read this book. Dear friends, I pray that what I have written will bring you great comfort, encouragement, and helpful direction as you seek to raise spiritually strong kids. Grace and peace to you!

NOTES

INTRODUCTION: PAINTING A PORTRAIT OF GOD'S STRENGTH AND LOVE

1. "New Research: Belief in Jesus Rises, Fueled by Younger Adults," Barna, April 7, 2025, https://www.barna.com/research/belief-in-jesus-rises/; "Modeling the Future of Religion in America," Pew Research Center, September 13, 2022, https://www.pewresearch.org/religion/2022/09/13/modeling-the-future-of-religion-in-america/.

CHAPTER 1: PARTNERS IN THE PROCESS

1. See 1 John 3:1-3; 1 John 4:7-12.
2. See Hebrews 12:2.
3. Charles Haddon Spurgeon, "Faith," sermon, December 14, 1856, The Spurgeon Center, https://www.spurgeon.org/resource-library/sermons/faith/#flipbook/.
4. Spurgeon, "Faith."
5. Spurgeon, "Faith."
6. Nicole B. Perry et al., "Childhood Self-Regulation as a Mechanism Through Which Early Overcontrolling Parents Is Associated with Adjustment in Preadolescence," *Developmental Psychology* 54, no. 8 (August 2018), 1542–1554, https://doi.org/10.1037/dev0000536.

CHAPTER 2: THE WISEST WAY

1. If you're interested in taking a deeper dive into this subject, study the beatitudes in Matthew 5:3-12.

CHAPTER 3: A HEALTHY PARENTING STYLE FOR A STRONG RELATIONSHIP

1. Jim Fay, *Helicopters, Drill Sergeants and Consultants* (Cline-Fay Institute, 1988).

CHAPTER 4: LOVING LIMITS

1. "Turn Your Words into Gold: The Art of Enforceable Statements," Love and Logic Institute, October 11, 2024, https://www.loveandlogic.com/blogs/our-blog/parenting-with-enforceable-statements.

CHAPTER 6: SERVING, CHORES, AND ALLOWANCE

1. Nancy Stewart, "Clean Up Song," 2010, https://nancymusic.com/SOM/2010/clean-up-song.htm.

CHAPTER 7: PRAYER, PLANNING, AND PATIENCE

1. Julia Schønning Vigdal and Kolbjørn Kallesten Brønnick, "A Systematic Review of 'Helicopter Parenting' and Its Relationship with Anxiety and Depression," *Frontiers in Psychology* 13 (May 24, 2022): 872981, https://doi.org/10.3389/fpsyg.2022.872981.
2. *Merriam-Webster Dictionary*, "sympathy," accessed December 10, 2025, https://www.merriam-webster.com/dictionary/sympathy.
3. *Merriam-Webster Dictionary*, "empathy," accessed December 10, 2025, https://www.merriam-webster.com/dictionary/empathy.

CHAPTER 8: GIVING THEM MOXIE AND MOTIVATION

1. "Modeling the Future of Religion in America," Pew Research Center, September 13, 2022, https://www.pewresearch.org/religion/2022/09/13/modeling-the-future-of-religion-in-america/.

CHAPTER 9: SMART STRATEGIES AROUND SMARTPHONES AND SCREENS

1. Ioannis Katsantonis and Ros McLellan, "The Role of Parent–Child Interactions in the Association Between Mental Health and Prosocial Behavior: Evidence from Early Childhood to Late Adolescence," *International Journal of Behavioral Development* 48, no. 1 (2023): 59–70, https://journals.sagepub.com/doi/10.1177/01650254231202444.
2. Jack Nicas and Zach Wichter, "A Worry for Some Pilots: Their Hands-On Flying Skills Are Lacking," *New York Times*, March 14, 2019, https://www.nytimes.com/2019/03/14/business/automated-planes.html.
3. Jill Sakai, "How Synaptic Pruning Shapes Neural Wiring During Development and, Possibly, in Disease," *PNAS* 117, no. 28 (June 24, 2020): 16096–16099, https://doi.org/10.1073/pnas.2010281117.
4. Jacquelyn Cafasso, "What Is Synaptic Pruning?" Healthline, updated September 18, 2018, https://www.healthline.com/health/synaptic-pruning.
5. Amrit Kaur Purba et al., "Social Media Use and Health Risk Behaviours in Young People: Systematic Review and Meta-Analysis," *BMJ* 383 (November 29, 2023): e073552, https://doi.org/10.1136/bmj-2022-073552; Roberta Pires Vasconcellos et al., "Electronic Screen Use and Children's Socioemotional Problems: A Systematic Review and Meta-Analysis of Longitudinal Studies," *Psychological Bulletin* 151, no. 5 (May 2025): 513–543, https://doi.org/10.1037/bul0000468; and Emily Young et al., "Frequent Social Media Use and Experiences with Bullying Victimization, Persistent Feelings of Sadness or Hopelessness, and Suicide Risk Among High School Students—Youth Risk Behavior Survey, United States, 2023," supplement, *Morbidity and Mortality Weekly Report* 73, no. S4 (October 10, 2024): 23–30, https://doi.org/10.15585/mmwr.su7304a3.
6. Sapien Labs, *Age of First Smartphone/Tablet and Mental Wellbeing Outcomes* (Global Mind Project, May 15 2023), 2, https://sapienlabs.org/wp-content/uploads/2023/05/Sapien-Labs-Age-of-First-Smartphone-and-Mental-Wellbeing-Outcomes.pdf.

7. "Media and Entertainment: Video Games Sector," International Trade Administration, accessed December 14, 2025, https://www.trade.gov/media-entertainment-video-games-sector; David Montgomery, "54% of Americans Read a Book This Year," YouGov, December 21, 2023, https://today.yougov.com/entertainment/articles/48239-54-percent-of-americans-read-a-book-this-year. According to the Census Bureau, the US population reached about 338.5 million in 2023. See census.gov/popclock.

CHAPTER 10: GOOD EXAMPLES AND RIGHT THINKING

1. Sandra Ackerman, "The Development and Shaping of the Brain" in *Discovering the Brain* (National Academies Press, 1992), https://www.ncbi.nlm.nih.gov/books/NBK234146/.
2. Gerry Leisman et al., "Emotional Brain Development: Neurobiological Indicators from Fetus Through Toddlerhood," *Brain Sciences* 15, no. 8 (August 8, 2025): 846, https://pmc.ncbi.nlm.nih.gov/articles/PMC12384854/pdf/brainsci-15-00846.pdf.
3. Charles Haddon Spurgeon, "The Best Donation," sermon, April 5, 1891, The Spurgeon Center, https://www.spurgeon.org/resource-library/sermons/the-best-donation/#flipbook/.

ABOUT THE AUTHOR

Charles Fay, PhD, is an internationally recognized author, consultant, and public speaker. He is also president of the Love and Logic Institute, which became part of Amen Clinics in 2020. Millions of educators, mental health professionals, and parents worldwide have benefited from Dr. Fay's down-to-earth solutions to the most common and frustrating behaviors displayed by youth of all ages, methods that come directly from years of research and clinical experience serving severely disturbed youth and their families in psychiatric hospitals, public and private schools, and homes.

Dr. Fay's interest in education and psychology was piqued by years of contact with some of our nation's most dynamic experts in these fields. This early exposure began in childhood when he participated in training events with his father, Jim Fay. Jim is one of the nation's leading experts on child discipline and has over fifty years of experience in public education. The internationally recognized Love and Logic approach was literally developed around Dr. Charles Fay as he grew. Now, he jokes, "I think that's why I became a psychologist . . . just to figure out what they were doing to me as a kid! But let me be clear . . . I absolutely adore my mom and dad as a result of these experiences."

Dr. Fay earned his PhD with highest honors from the University of South Carolina. Prior to and during his university training in school and clinical psychology, he enjoyed working with children in psychiatric, public school, and mental health settings. Because of his high-powered sense of humor and storytelling skills, audiences experience the most memorable and life-changing form of learning—learning that's mentally connected to joy and real-life examples.

Dr. Fay and his wife, Monica, reside in the mountains outside Denver, Colorado. They have three sons who are young adults. When Dr. Fay isn't writing, consulting, or speaking, he enjoys snowmobiling, off-road motorcycle riding, hiking, and other active sports with his family. To learn more about Dr. Fay and the Love and Logic approach, visit loveandlogic.com.